lf

and

nent

in association with  The Telegraph **BUSINESSCLUB**

teach yourself®

change and
crisis management
james b. rieley

For over 60 years, more than
50 million people have learnt over
750 subjects the **teach yourself**
way, with impressive results.

be where you want to be
with **teach yourself**

in association with

The publisher has used its best endeavours to ensure that the URLs for external websites referred to in this book are correct and active at the time of going to press. However, the publisher and the author have no responsibility for the websites and can make no guarantee that a site will remain live or that the content will remain relevant, decent or appropriate.

For UK order enquiries: please contact Bookpoint Ltd, 130 Milton Park, Abingdon, Oxon OX14 4SB. Telephone: +44 (0) 1235 827720. Fax: +44 (0) 1235 400454. Lines are open 09.00–17.00, Monday to Saturday, with a 24-hour message answering service. Details about our titles and how to order are available at www.teachyourself.co.uk

Long renowned as the authoritative source for self-guided learning – with more than 50 million copies sold worldwide – the **teach yourself** series includes over 500 titles in the fields of languages, crafts, hobbies, business, computing and education.

British Library Cataloguing in Publication Data: a catalogue record for this title is available from the British Library.

ISBN-10: 0 340 928328
ISBN-13: 978 0340 928325

First published 2006

This edition published 2006.

The **teach yourself** name is a registered trade mark of Hodder Headline.

Typeset by Servis Filmsetting Ltd, Manchester.
Printed in Great Britain for Hodder Education, a division of Hodder Headline, 338 Euston Road, London NW1 3BH, by Cox & Wyman Ltd, Reading, Berkshire.

Hodder Headline's policy is to use papers that are natural, renewable and recyclable products and made from wood grown in sustainable forests. The logging and manufacturing processes are expected to conform to the environmental regulations of the country of origin.

Impression number   10 9 8 7 6 5 4 3 2 1

Year   2010 2009 2008 2007 2006

Dedication

Surviving change and crisis is a function of sound decision-making

contents

	preface	xi
Part 1	**introduction**	**1**
01	**change and crises in organizations**	**3**
	how change occurs	7
	how crises can occur	7
	creating an environment for change	10
02	**what change is all about**	**17**
	enabling change	22
	avoiding inappropiate addiction	28
Part 2	**stories from the office**	**37**
03	**how decisions impact change**	**39**
	the quick fix is still alive and well	40
	where has all the talent gone?	42
	choking on success?	44
	choices, bloody choices	47
	when is fast, fast enough?	49
	wicked, wicked problems	51
	leading by example	59
	when teams go bad	61
	gaining commitment or getting compliance	65

04	**how our beliefs impact change**	**67**
	another shark in formaldehyde?	68
	risk prevention, lesson 1	70
	it's a matter of perspective	72
	putting ticks in boxes?	74
	deciding who you are	77
	the manager as coach	79
	the onset of panjandrums	82
	good news, bad news	85
	too busy to see the oncoming train?	88
05	**dealing with influencing factors**	**91**
	communications: art or science?	92
	trying to stay dry	96
	events dear boy, events	98
	what do they expect will occur?	100
	oh, the money thing	102
Part 3	**stories from the workplace**	**105**
06	**getting the work done and surviving**	**107**
	getting their heads around what it is like	108
	why things don't get done	109
	realizing the potential of teams	112
	one from column A and one from column B?	114
	orderly transitions	117
07	**finding out what we don't know**	**120**
	knowing what we don't know	121
	how incentives can go wrong	123
	the brainstorming debate	127
	robbing Peter to pay Paul?	130
	the perfect storm of impending crisis	133
08	**being competent to survive it all**	**138**
	understanding alignment gaps	139
	dealing with stress in the workplace	143
	rushing to nowhere?	148

	missing the signals?	150
	skilled incompetence: is it still alive?	153
	have you tied your own hands?	155
Part 4	**structures and worksheets**	**159**
09	**structures that impact performance**	**161**
	the downside of stepping in	162
	the problems with the 'quick-fix'	163
	dealing with the hiring conundrum	165
	changing mental models	167
	pressure: the risk of backfiring	169
	prioritizing investment decisions: training	171
	identifying structural tension	173
10	**worksheets**	**176**
	left-hand column	177
	an alignment matrix	181
	knowing when to let go	184
	ladder of inference	187
	what are we doing?	189
	how to help behaviours change	193
	summary	**197**
	index	**199**

preface

The subject of small and medium enterprises (SMEs) is a tad complex, and because of that, when beginning to work on this project, it seemed to make all the sense in the world to talk to as many people as I could who either have SMEs, work for SMEs, or have worked for SMEs. It was at this point I realized that many of their stories provide tremendous insights as to some of the challenges of ongoing change and how to avoid potential organizational crises.

It also made sense to avoid having this book end up like so many of the business books that are published each year – sitting on a shelf trying to look impressive. Being a retired owner CEO of an SME for over 24 years, I realized that this book should be written in a way that readers can actually *learn from* and *apply* the information, beginning the day they open it up. And consequently, this volume of the *Teach Yourself* series is meant to help managers and employees of organizations from all sectors, and of all sizes, avoid the problems associated with ongoing change and crises. The ability to manage change and crises can make the difference between organizational survival (and prosperity) and a steady downward decline in organizational effectiveness.

This volume is divided into four parts, with Parts 1 and 4 being devoted to practical examples of how to avoid the problems, and Parts 2 and 3 comprising short stories that highlight some of the dynamics that organizations face when dealing with change and crises.

Part 2 – *Stories from the Office* – includes key stories that highlight some of the challenges facing SME management; Part 3 – *Stories from the Workplace* – includes key stories that highlight some of the challenges facing front-line workers; Part 4 –

Structures and worksheets – includes in-depth lessons of how to avoid problems that plague SMEs, and reproducible worksheets that readers can use to help them take the ambiguity out of the decision-making process.

Laced throughout Part 1, the introductory chapters, there are causal loop diagrams, used here to provide some clarity as to some of the dynamics involved around the impact of change on organizations and their respective populations. Whilst to some the causal loop diagrams may appear to add confusion to an already confusing topic, by following the arrows and small 'directional' identifying symbols ('s' and 'o'), one can actually 'see' what is occurring or can occur. The 's's denote a change in the 'same' direction – more causes more, or less causes less of the next variable in the diagram. The 'o's represent an 'opposite' reaction – more of one variable causes less of the next, or less of one variable causes more of the next.

One last thing . . . when I was planning this book, I thought it would be helpful to include the 'worksheet' section, but then the logistical issue arose of how to ensure that the readers of the book could access full size copies of the templates in the book. These templates are available to purchasers of Change and Crisis Management at www.rieley.com, Resources link.

My hope is that you, the reader, can use this book, *Change and Crisis Management*, to help you and your organization realize its potential. In business, there really is nothing more important.

Dr James B. Rieley
jbrieley@rieley.com
www.rieley.com

As I have said before, I don't know of a single author who can honestly claim to have 'done it all', and because of this belief, I would like to thank

Richard Smith,
for his commitment, continuous support and countless contributions;

Richard Collins,
whose commitment and support for the project has been unbelievable;

Patricia Kreiter and the STOL Group,
for creating a very special practice field;

Angus Lyon, Becky Alsup-Kingery, Miles Rees, Ratimir Janekovic, Addy Kelle and Francis Lambert
for their insightful contributions;

Alison Frecknall and Jill Birch,
for always believing;

Dr Keith Roberts,
for years of support and guidance

and

Angelina,
for being the ongoing inspiration for it all.

part 1

introduction

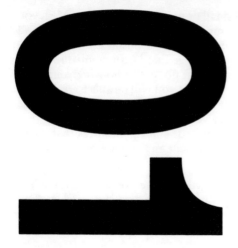

01

change and
crises in
organizations

In this chapter you will learn:

- how change and crises occur
  in organizations
- how to create a positive
  environment for change

If you own or work for a small or medium enterprise (SME), you know that, whilst your company is probably more flexible and adaptable to changing dynamics in the business environment, you don't have some of the leverage that larger companies have. Fair enough, but the reality is that no matter how big your business is, size does not guarantee that you will be able to realize the potential of it. As a matter of fact, size doesn't even guarantee that your company will survive indefinitely. The only thing that any business can do to help provide some guarantees that it can survive is to ensure that management and employees make better decisions.

Many years ago, I ran an SME. Those were the days when I would have identified my business with adjectives such as *flexible*, *agile*, *responsive*, *innovative* and *fun*. But admittedly, these weren't the only adjectives I lived with. I also had *stress*, *panic* and *pressure* to live with. The only way I was able to be successful was to create an environment in which the first set of adjectives became the ones that made a difference.

Regardless of what anyone says about the mission of his or her business being to do marvellous altruistic things, the real bottom line of business is to make money . . . and to make more of it than you spend. This means making the right decisions, at the right times, for the right reasons, and reducing the chances for problems. And in the process of learning how to do these things, I learnt quite a few lessons.

Lesson 1: Ensure that all your employees have the same basic picture you have for the future of the company. The ability to have a clear picture of where you want your organization to go in the future is important, but making sure that all the employees can see the same picture is critical. If your employees *don't* have the same picture you do, when faced with options, they may make a decision that will take you off track. And then the chances that your company will become the company you want it to become will be diminished dramatically.

Lesson 2: Have a good idea of what scenarios your company will encounter as it grows. Too often, we don't pay enough attention to what we may encounter as we try to grow a company. Paying attention to what your competitors are doing, what regulations may be put in force, and what your customers may need or want in the future can provide you with insights as to the decisions you will need if you are to stay on track and continue to grow your company.

Lesson 3: Build alignment and commitment to your organizational goals. One way to get things done in an organization is to keep pressure on your employees to deliver; but this results in wasted time, resources, and efforts to keep everyone focused on the right things. A better way is to create an environment in which your employees *want* to do the right things, at the right times, for the right reasons. Gaining commitment always results in better value than driving compliance.

Lesson 4: Have a plan. It is surprising how many CEOs of SMEs don't have a *real* plan on how to grow their companies. A sound plan begins with a clear vision of where you want to go, and from that picture a set of actions are developed that will ensure that the goals are achieved. And regardless of what some consultancies may try to sell you; a good plan is nothing more than common sense, and it is something that you can do yourself.

Lesson 5: Identify contingency actions for when things don't go as planned. Many of the companies that *do* have plans forget to identify what they will need to do if something runs amok; and the cardinal rule of business is that if something can run amok, it will. Identify what could go wrong, and then build mini-plans to deal with those contingencies.

Lesson 6: Appreciate the efforts of your employees. I don't know of a single successful CEO who really believes that his (or her) company's success has been achieved without employees. You can have all the latest technology; you can have an endless cheque book; and you can have absolutely no competition; but without your people, there is no way you can achieve your vision. And if your employees don't feel that you appreciate all the efforts they are contributing, they will cease to contribute, and then you will be stuck.

Lesson 7: Test your decisions before you make them. Testing decisions need not delay the decision-making process, but will ensure that the decisions you make will be the most appropriate. Identify what you need to do, then determine *what else* will happen when you implement your decision. The whole issue of identifying potential unintended consequences of decisions can be a major lever to ensure that what you *want* to happen will happen.

Lesson 8: Prioritize learning for yourself and your employees. It has been often stated that one of the key differentiators for organizational success is *how much and how fast your people can learn.*

Change and Crisis Management has been developed and written to address these and other issues that cause many SME owners, chief-executives, managers, and employees to stay awake at night.

This is a book that is filled with opportunity: opportunity to create an environment in which your company can realize its potential . . . and with it, survive as long as you want it to.

According to a google.com search I did before beginning to write this book, there are 48,200,000 available 'hits' for change and crisis management. I suppose I could have received permission and just liberally quoted from any of the almost 50 million entries, but instead, I decided to opt out for a common-sense approach.

There has been quite a bit of good information written about how to deal with change, and how to deal with organizational crises, but the reality is that quite a bit of it is about as complicated as the problems are themselves. No, common sense, and in plain talk, seems to be the most rational approach.

First, why another book on change and crisis management? Other than being asked to write it by the publisher, it is clear that the whole issue of how to manage through change and crisis is still a problem for many organizations. The reason is that it can be a bit complicated.

The elements of change include not only the odd change initiatives that seem to be pervasive in organizations today, but also include such elements as the willingness and ability of managers and employees to evolve the way in which they interpret management messages; their willingness and ability to accept those messages; and the skill sets they may have to enable them to demonstrate the behaviours that the change initiative brings. And if all that doesn't complicate the issue enough, think about this.

When, in your best memory, can you recall that a crisis was commonly understood? Yes, impending bankruptcy can generate a common understanding that a crisis is upon an organization. Yes, when exogenous events such as the recent upward spiral of oil prices can drive expenses through the roof, managers and employees of a company under that kind of pressure might agree that it is a crisis. But in most cases, the term 'crisis' is much akin to the term 'art' – it is in the eye of the beholder. This statement is not to diminish the fact that crises do occur in organizations, but the point is that it can be difficult to avoid or deal with a crisis if not everyone in the organization perceives it to be one.

The only thing for sure is that if crises are not avoided or dealt with effectively, and if change doesn't become something that we get our collective heads around, there will be few organizations that will ever realize their potential.

How change occurs

It doesn't.

Change in organizations is like fish in water. Go ask any fish what water is, and they won't know. (Okay, I know you can't actually ask a fish anything, but work with me on this metaphor.) The reason fish don't know what water is is because it *is* the environment they live in. And even though academics and consultants and many organizational personnel would say the same holds true for organizations and change, many of us still think (or would like to think) that change comes and goes.

I tend to believe that this is largely due to our own organizational preoccupation with trying to implement 'change programmes' and speaking of change as if change only occurs when management thinks it needs to. The reality is that every minute of every day of every year, change is taking place in our companies. I am not even sure that we can manage change. Managing change implies that we can control it, and clearly we can't, we can only learn to deal with it as effectively as possible.

So for those readers who bought this book to find answers on how to keep the status quo and all that we think it can bring . . . get over it.

How crises can occur

Organizational crises can occur in various ways, and one of the reasons that we don't see them coming is that many senior managers tend to look at things in a linear fashion – we make decisions, we obtain funding, we implement specific initiatives, the employees carry them out, and our organizational performance improves. Okay, on paper that is fine, but the reality of business is that for every action, there is a reaction and you cannot see this through linear thinking. By looking at the implications of

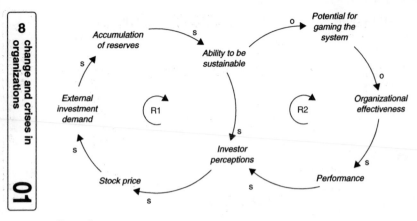

Figure 1

business decisions in a more systemic way, it is possible to see the 'what else might happen' before it happens. And if you can do this, you can stave off organizational crises. The systemic diagrams, Figures 1–3, show how this is done. But something worth remembering: most crises occur because we cause them to occur.

In Figure 1 there are two loops. Loop R1 identifies a standard structure: the more your organization is able to be sustainable, the better the perceptions of investors are. This in turn tends to increase your stock price, which drives up investor demand, generating more revenues, which gives you a greater ability to be sustainable. This loop shows that 'more leads to more', which in the normal view of business is good news. Loop R2 shows how the dynamic behaviours of loop R1 are reinforced. As the organization is more sustainable, there is less of a potential that the employees will decide to game the organizational systems. As the potential for gaming the system decreases, the result is higher organizational effectiveness, which leads to better performance, which will increase even further the perceptions of investors in the company. Again, more leads to more.

Now before I go on, it is important to note that the whole belief that 'more leads to more', although it can be good news, as seen in these diagrams, it can also be bad news. More customer complaints can lead to more frustrations on the part of customer service staff people, which can lead to more customer complaints. Therefore, 'more leading to more' being considered good news is only appropriate if the 'more' that is being seen is good to begin with.

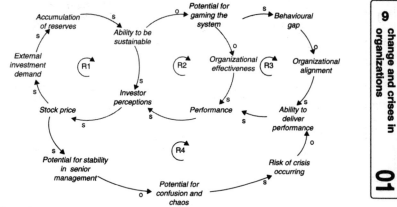

Figure 2

Back to the story of why crises can occur. If for some reason managers and employees do decide to begin gaming the organizational system, the whole structure becomes bad news. The onset of gaming the system means that there will be a behavioural gap between what is needed, and what is actually seen (see Figure 2). This leads to less organizational alignment and a corresponding lessening in the organization's ability to deliver high performance. A reduced ability to deliver performance results in reduced performance, which will cause potential investors to not think kindly of placing their funds with you, reducing the stock price. A faltering stock price can reduce the potential for a stable senior management group, which leads to an increased potential for confusion and chaos on the part of the employees, increasing the risk of a crisis, reducing the ability to perform even further. The entire organizational performance structure has turned horribly wrong, simply because one of the structural variables has gone bad.

Another way that a crisis can occur is when a new (but not well thought out) strategy is tried to be implemented. The ineffective strategy saps cash reserves, which . . . well, just follow the arrows around in Figure 3. Again, the 'good news' structure has now turned to 'bad news', and a crisis can loom on the horizon. This last example was seen by all of us during the demise of Marconi. It is a pity that the key decision-makers didn't see it before they went ahead with their strategic shift.

By using systemic thinking, it is possible to see 'what else might happen' before it happens, thus helping to create an environment in which crises do not need to occur.

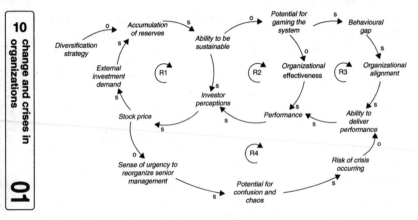

Figure 3

Creating an environment for change

The first line of Charles Dickens' *A Tale of Two Cities* sums up the feelings about most organizational change efforts – 'It was the best of times, it was the worst of times'. In most organizations that have undertaken large-scale change initiatives, there is a vast chasm between those who support the change efforts and those who don't. This chasm can have a dramatic impact on the outcome of the change efforts. A seemingly un-discussable question that relates directly to this is, *'what makes those who support organizational change efforts believe that they are right?'*

There has been extensive research in recent years on change initiatives. Much of this research has focused on the issues of the timing of the change, the type of change, or the rationale for the change. I would propose, however, that these issues are relatively low-leverage areas for examination. Additionally, I would suggest that by looking at these issues, we take a myopic, non-systemic view of some of the underlying issues behind change. By looking at the issues of timing, type, or rationale for change, we are looking only at the tip of the iceberg, and if we are to understand better the dynamics of change, we need to look deeper, to the inherent structural beliefs that we hold regarding to change. These beliefs are found in the stories of our organizations, and by reflecting on these stories, we will have the ability to understand some of the systemic dynamics of change.

The country that has shown the greatest shift in how business is conducted is the United States. In the late 18th century, the US underwent dramatic change. This change was driven by the widespread belief that our 'community' was not being treated fairly by the central authority force of the community. The community was comprised of a cross-sectional group of people with many common traits. Some of these common traits included: the desire to improve the quality of life, the desire to live in peace, and the desire to control individual and collective destinies. These common traits brought many of these people together over a period of several hundred years, and over time the belief that the population was not being treated fairly grew. In the late 1770s, the growth of this belief stimulated a response to the authority and the American Revolution ensued.

As more and more of the population became convinced that they were being treated unfairly by the government in place (the authority), the pressure for change increased. The change in government caused the feeling of unfair treatment to mitigate, and therefore, reduced the pressure to change. The growth of collective feelings of unfair treatment was enabled by a shared set of values that included the mental model that the government in place was made up of people who were 'different' from the population as a whole. Additionally, people who were not directly connected to the government, but who also did not share the feeling of unfair treatment, were also considered to be different. It is this separation of people that begins to set in motion another dynamic, the dynamic of the assumption that there is a 'right' answer.

To support the assumption that there is a 'right' answer requires binary thinking, and our language contributes to this type of thinking. When thinking in binary terms, we become trapped by our language to believe that things are either 'hot' or 'cold', 'open' or 'closed', 'smart' or 'dumb', 'good' or 'bad', 'right' or 'wrong,' and 'us' or 'them'. When being in a culture that supports this type of language usage, it is relatively easy to see how 'we' can have the 'right' answer, and therefore, 'they' must surely be 'bad', as 'they' don't subscribe to the same set of assumptions.

Historically, we have seen this same dynamic at play many times. Examples of this belief abound – the many wars we have been in, labour strikes, the Communist 'witch-hunts' of the 1950s, and the many efforts to implement change in organizations. In all these scenarios, the common denominator is the belief that there is a 'right' thing to do. Therefore, the question might be 'why is it so difficult for us to convince others that we are right?'

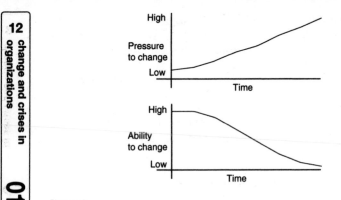

Figure 4

In organizations today, there is a move to change due to one or more pressures: the increase in competition, the decrease in available resources, the increase in demands for accountability, the acceleration in the development of technology, and the demands of stakeholders for higher returns on investment. The 'rule' is, the greater the pressure for change, the greater the inability to cope with change (see Figure 4).

All of these pressures can lead to the assumption that there could be a better way to manage an organization, to deal with the ability to cope with the pressures. The difficulty lies in several places. Some managers deal with the pressures by believing that the previously stated pressures should not affect their ability to manage; some managers believe that the pressures will subside; some managers believe that the pressures are not real. In all of these cases, these managers risk becoming at odds with the move to change. This begins to set up the fractionalizing belief that some managers are 'right' and some are 'wrong'. This fractionalization of an organization, no matter how severe, will begin to reduce the organizational potential to be effective over time. This will, in itself, put increasing pressure on the organization for change.

As Figure 5 shows, the inside loop demonstrates a reinforcing behaviour – as the pressure to change increases, the belief in fairness of authority decreases, and as the belief in fairness of authority decreases, the pressure to change increases. This dynamic is largely due to the fact that change is seen as a mandate, not a choice. In the outside loop, as the pressure to change increases, the risk of fractionalization increases, this in turn reduces

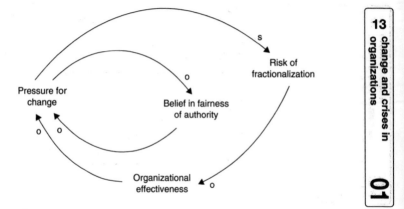

Figure 5

organizational effectiveness, which in turn increases the pressure for change. This set of dynamics is also reinforcing behaviours and will cause additional risk of fractionalization, reduction of effectiveness, and increased pressure for change.

As we have learned from history, there is more effort expended into establishing the 'rightness' of change initiatives than there is in building alignment for dealing with change. It is this belief in the rightness of actions to deal with change that causes much of the chaos in organizations today, leading to reduced potential for effectiveness over time.

By forcing the issue of 'we are right', we, by default, are stating that those who disagree with the methods to deal with change are wrong and, therefore, of less value to the organization. By establishing the mental model of some people being of less value, we create more fractionalization and, again, less potential for effectiveness over time.

When examining the dynamics shown in Figure 6, we need to think about which of the variables shown are the most important to the employees, administration, customers, suppliers and stakeholders of the organization. There are few organizations that feel that being right is more important than being effective. If the focus is on being right, the strategies are relatively simple – put forth the message that only certain people will be allowed to make decisions due to the fact that no one else is competent to make them. This message, however, will set the loops spinning, albeit in a way that will fractionalize the organization. There is ample

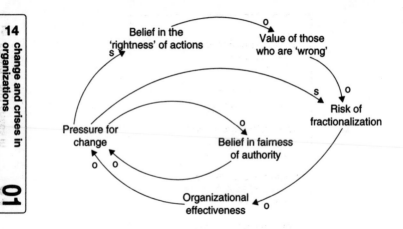

Figure 6

evidence that this message will additionally dilute the organizational climate by damaging morale, reducing risk taking, and consequently, reducing its potential for effectiveness. If the organization is more concerned about increasing its effectiveness over time, the strategies are a little more complex.

First, the organization and its leadership need to be very clear about its rationale and expectations for change. These expectations should be put in the context of the organizational mission and purpose. Without this clarity as to the rationale and expectations for change, the organizational population will begin to fall into chaos and confusion and become fractionalized.

The rationale should include a systemic view of the organization today, as well as a systemic view of what the future could bring. This view should be developed based on the ramifications of change due to the many external forces that impact the organization (see Figure 7).

It is an understanding of these driving forces that enables an organization to be able more clearly to articulate its expectations of change and how it will affect the organizational mission and purposes.

Included in the expectations should be timelines that articulate at what point the organization will need to be at a specific time. This is analogous to the need to plan rest stops on a long journey: If we are to see six cities in six days, we need to plan the journey to be able to arrive in a new city each day. This is important so

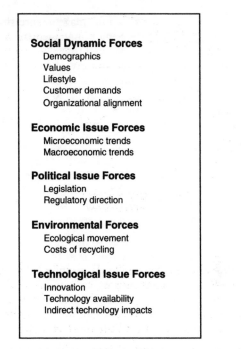

Social Dynamic Forces
Demographics
Values
Lifestyle
Customer demands
Organizational alignment

Economic Issue Forces
Microeconomic trends
Macroeconomic trends

Political Issue Forces
Legislation
Regulatory direction

Environmental Forces
Ecological movement
Costs of recycling

Technological Issue Forces
Innovation
Technology availability
Indirect technology impacts

Figure 7

that everyone involved in the change process can begin to formulate their individual plans for dealing with the changes.

Second, a plan to help enhance the skill sets of the employees should be made visible. For every change, there is the potential that different skill sets than those currently in use will be needed by the organizational population. The skill set enhancement programme – series of courses developed to target the specific skills that the employees will need to be effective in the organization as well as contribute to the overall organizational effectiveness – should include options for all employees. It should be recognized that all employees means *all* employees. Senior management of the organization should be the first to participate in the training programmes for two reasons.

1   In a time when we are all talking about the concept of leadership vs. management, it is critical to understand that leadership is all about creating an environment in which the organizational population can learn how to be more effective over time.

Management, however, is all about making sure that people do what they are supposed to do. Senior 'management' became senior management because it was assumed that they knew best how to do their jobs. Regardless of the validity of that decision process, being at the top of the organizational food chain does not, and should not, imply that the person, or persons, knows everything. An organization that is interested in becoming more effective needs to be open to ongoing learning – at all levels.

2   If an organizational population receives the signal that senior management is not participating in skill enhancement offerings, the message will be that they shouldn't have to either. Participation in skill enhancement is clearly a matter of 'do as I do', not 'do as I say'. Participation in skill enhancement can be, and should be, tied to individual performance review assessments for all managers.

Third, the organization will need to monitor the ongoing change process. This is important to ensure that the internal population that is being impacted by change is moving forward at both an appropriate level of understanding and an appropriate schedule.

Fourth, the management tools that can have the greatest impact on organizational effectiveness are non-traditional. Most often, the tools management uses to ensure alignment and the meeting of expectations include resource allocation, economic incentives, and a clearly defined organizational structure. In an organization focused on effectiveness, the appropriate tools include engagement, explanation and expectation clarity. With the application of these tools, employees are more apt to take ownership for the long-term success of the organization.

It should be remembered that dealing with change effectively requires that the organization create an environment conducive to allowing change to occur in an orderly manner. This is not to imply that change must be structured; in fact, most change is not planned. Change happens in organizations because it needs to happen. The issue for senior management or leadership is to ensure that the change efforts do not debilitate the organization by evolving into a fight over who is right, who is in step with the new organization direction, and who wants the organization to be effective over time. We all want our organizations to become more effective; creating a positive environment to deal with change can assist in this process. Developing positive environments for change can be win–win situations for organizations; all we have to do is look at lessons learned from history.

what change is all about

In this chapter you will learn:

- how organizations have arrived where they are
- how to enable successful change
- how to make a rationale for change efforts
- how to avoid becoming addicted to change

When I was a young boy, I was relatively unaware of the impacts of change in organizations. My father owned his own business and would talk about what was going on at the office, but I never really realized how change was affecting how he did what he did. As I grew older, I started working for my father, and when I was barely a teenager, I started to see organizational change. The small business would get orders from customers, we would make the parts they ordered, we would ship them, and then the cycle would hopefully start over again. His employees rarely changed – they came to work each day and fabricated plastic parts as best they could with the old, sometimes not very well maintained, equipment. Technology had made little impact in those days. Every several years we would buy a new machine, but in reality the new machine was only new to us as my father believed that a pre-owned machine would work as well as a new one; and in many cases, better. The technology behind the machines hadn't really changed in many years.

When given the opportunity, I became the business owner. It was then that I started to realize the impacts of change in an organizational climate framework. This could have been a combination of my increased awareness (driven largely by the necessity to become more aware as the person who had full organizational responsibility), but also due to the times. It was the early 1970s and events began to change the way in which Americans looked at business. The oil embargo, the onslaught of technology advances, the rush for businesses to grow through acquisition, and our awareness of how we treat people all impacted the way in which we did, or didn't, do business. These factors all impacted the way in which we ran our organizations, the way we made decisions. They also changed our lives and the future of our organizations.

The oil embargo of 1974 created the need to begin to shift how we looked at the world. Suddenly, the all-powerful West was virtually at the mercy of a handful of small countries that just happened to control a resource that we depended upon. No longer would we be able to expect inexpensive (in relative terms to the rest of the world) fuel supplies to run our cars, heat our homes, and supply our energy needs for our businesses. This change, or more importantly, its impact, was something that seemed to come out of the blue – we, as a population, didn't expect or anticipate it. In 1974 I was the new CEO of our business, a plastics fabricating business. As all plastics come from either natural gas or oil, a major shift in gas or oil prices could result in a major shift in the cost of the raw materials that we used in my company. It did, and it did. Seemingly overnight, the cost of fuel went from roughly 35 cents per gallon to almost a dollar per gallon, and the price of plastic raw materials followed suit. This was my first business crisis and required a shift in how I viewed the business; after all, change can be both good news and bad news at the same time. In many cases, the difference between good news and bad news is simply how one looks at the impact of the change.

For my company, the bad news was that my direct costs went up dramatically. In a relatively competitive environment, when the cost of materials increases, the ability to become more effective in fabricating those materials becomes more important. Bad news – raw materials cost increased; good news – we became more innovative. Some of my competitors were hit harder than we were due to their imbalance between material costs and labour costs. Bad news – some friends went out of business; good news – some competitors went out of business. As the cost of materials increased, our ability to be effective would need to increase due to the increasing cost of 'sloppiness' in how we conducted the business of fabricating plastic parts to customers' tolerances. Bad news – our margin of error would be decreasing; good news – we would have to become more effective if we were to survive. As our materials cost was increasing, our need to have a happy, productive workforce was increasing. This was due to our perceived unwillingness to operate a plastics company with a revolving door at the employment office. Bad news – I would have to turn over more control of the day-to-day decision-making to the employees; good news – they knew better what decisions would be the most effective in helping them become more productive over time.

Were the changes the oil embargo forced upon us bad overall or good overall? I am not sure it is important to try to classify things into strictly built structures with titles of 'good' or 'bad'. In many cases, and mine in particular, the oil embargo of 1974 produced far more positive effects than negative ones. This is partially due to a mental model that 'good' and 'bad' is the same picture viewed from different perspectives. But also, it is due to my belief that the things I learned during that time enabled me to become better at what I did. This is a function of being open to exploring, open to learning, open to enabling an effective change process.

As the 1970s quickly moved through our time windows, technology achieved a duality in purpose. Technology was an agent of change, whilst at the same time, it caused change to occur.

In the late 1970s I purchased my first business fax machine. This machine seemed at the time to be a luxury – I only had one customer that I knew of that had a facsimile machine – but I reasoned that if I had the machine, I might save a trip or two to the customer's office. Although the customer was located less than two miles from my office, the idea seemed great at the time. I bought the machine, relatively archaic by today's standards, and it changed the way in which we were able to do business. I discovered that other customers of mine and suppliers to my company also had facsimile machines. This reduced our transaction time by almost 80 per cent. No longer were we locked into mailing in orders for raw materials, or mailing out changes to work drawings. Suddenly we could receive off-the-shelf materials in one-third of the time; we could get customer authorizations for changes approval requests in minutes instead of days. This made a dramatic impact on how we were able to meet customer needs. The computer, and its acquisition for business purposes did the same – less transaction time equalled higher effectiveness in meeting customer needs, or in other terms, organizational success.

The 1970s also saw an onslaught on the belief that organizational growth was a function of better planning, better strategies, better implementation, and better products or services. This was the birth of the age of acquisition as a growth strategy. No longer would an organization have to wait to grow, it could be done seemingly overnight. If you wanted to grow your company by 50 per cent, simply buy a company that had 50 per cent of your size, and wham, your company is now bigger. If you wanted 100 per cent growth, buy one that was equal to yours in size. The reality was that the resultant organizations were actually bigger – they were bigger in sales, in product lines, in number of employees, in debt, and in complexity. This was another example of the good news–bad news paradox. By becoming bigger through acquisition, an organization could achieve its goals for size, but by becoming bigger by acquisition, the potential to retain those gains was mitigated by the increase in complexity. Additional, and clearly unintended consequences of growth by acquisition, was the change in how we treated our employees. No longer was there a belief in the concept of 'lifetime employment'. Now, it seemed as if the organization's theme in dealing with employees was moving toward 'what have you done for me lately'. As more employees sensed the apparent shift in organizational thinking, they became more conscious of the importance of their role in the company. As some companies began to 'discard' employees who were not able to meet the current needs or standards of the company relating to productivity or potential productivity, they began to see positive results. Fewer employees meant fewer expenses, less expenses led to higher profits, or at least the potential to offset some of the immense debt incurred in the acquisition process. Unfortunately, the gains realized were only short term.

Many companies had embarked on a process of 'weeding out' the older, more expensive employees. The reasoning at the time seemed reasonable – let go the employees who made the highest salaries as a way to cut expenses. This, in most cases, meant the employees who were the oldest and had been at the company the longest. Remember, the prevailing culture until this time was one in which lifetime employment in an organization was the norm. As the older, longer tenured employees disappeared, organizations began to notice that along with the disappearance of relatively high cost employees was the disappearance of organizational memory. The employees that had worked for many years in an organization might not have had access to the latest business theory, but they were the repositories of information about how the organization 'really' functioned. This organizational memory had been built over time, and was lost almost overnight. Lost was the knowledge about what had been tried in the past and succeeded and/or failed. Lost was the understanding of how to 'get things done'. Lost was much of the history and, consequently, the cultural basis for an organization. Was this all bad? Lost memory of how an organization functions gave forth an opportunity to develop newer processes, newer policies and procedures, and newer strategies. Lost organizational memory enables an organization not to be frozen by perceived fear of what worked in the past and what didn't work. Lost understanding of 'how to get things done' can create an environment to do things in new ways. These are all examples of the duality of good news–bad news, and the opportunity to explore options as to how to deal with change.

It is the beginning of the twenty-first century and the impact of change is not much different now than it was in the 1970s. The way in which we deal with the cost of energy is still driving many organizations. The lessons of the 1970s of trying to avoid energy dependence on other, sometimes, vaguely friendly countries, have failed miserably. We currently import more oil than we did 25 years ago by a huge margin. This can result in many impacts on our organizations and people in the near and distant future. The rapid, almost daily changes in technology are enough to give us the sensation of being on a merry-go-round that is going faster and faster. In the late 1970s, a fax machine cost about £400 – today, you can get your faxes delivered automatically with your email for a few pounds per year. In the 1970s, we mailed everything via the Royal Mail Post – today, email (unheard of 25 years ago) is used by almost every organization that wants to succeed. In the late 1970s, cellular phones cost thousands of pounds, plus high airtime rates – today, you can get a phone for free and airtime rates are highly competitive. In the 1970s, it was believed that if you work hard, you will have a job for life – today the average person will work for eight companies in their lifetime. In the 1970s, an impressive merger may have meant a transaction of £300,000,000.00 and an impact on 1,000 people – today, it is merger transactions in excess of £5,000,000,000.00 and impacts on thousands of people in many countries.

With this apparent acceleration of change here today, and a pervasive belief that it will accelerate even further, an appropriate question might be, 'how can we become more effective at dealing with change?' I believe that an effective strategy to deal with change is to shift our thinking from, 'we have to deal with change' to 'how can we enable change to occur that has more of a positive impact on our lives?'

Enabling change

When change occurs, its effects impact many things. Very many things.

Our educational process has taught us several things about how to become successful. First, we have been taught that success is having the 'right' answer. Second, it is important to get the answer quickly. Third, we will measure success through quantitative means. When I was growing up, those things were driven into me at my school, in my home, and by my peers. There is a shift in how we are looking at success in today's world.

It is becoming increasingly clear that there is a direct connection between having the right answer and being able to understand the question. This, on the surface, appears to be common sense.

In the world of business today, however, we rarely take the time to really understand. Stockholder pressures, competitive pressures, and transaction time decreases have caused us to try to work faster to get the right answer faster. By developing a better understanding of the question, our solutions, our answers, will be richer, more robust, and more appropriate. Applying systems dynamics to questions can provide an opportunity to increase our understanding.

Systems thinking, or systems dynamics, is a mindset, a way of thinking. Begun in the 1950s by Jay Forester in his work at MIT, systems dynamics consists of a set of theories and tools that can enable one to explore the relationships between variable issues that face our organizations. In 1990, Peter Senge authored *The Fifth Discipline*, a book that furthered the use and understanding about systems dynamics. In his book, Senge talks about the five disciplines of learning: Personal Mastery, Mental Models, Team Learning, Shared Vision and Systems Thinking. According to Senge, systems thinking is all about understanding the patterns of relationships between things and either changing or reinforcing those relationships to achieve better organizational outcomes. It was *The Fifth Discipline* that introduced many to the concept of causal loops, behaviour over time charts, and systems archetypes. When exploring how organizations can deal better with change, using systems thinking can provide high leverage to understand the dynamics of change in an organization.

Some of the issues revolving around organizational change include the culture of an organization (organizational climate), the age of the organizational population, the length of employment in the organization of the population, the type of change, the frequency of change, the level of and effectiveness of organizational communications, and the ability of the organizational population to see the rationale for the change. All of these factors are interrelated. No longer can the senior management of an organization simply decide to implement a change effort without understanding these relationships, unless they are prepared for the potential for the development of ongoing organizational defences that will mitigate any change efforts.

There are several considerations to explore when contemplating the implementation of an organizational change effort. The first of these considerations is 'what are we trying to accomplish?' In many organizations, either direct or indirect external forces drive change. Regardless of the impetus for change, it is crucial to

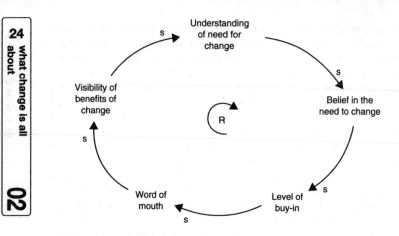

Figure 8

reflect on what the outcome of the change effort would be. Does the organization want to change what it does, or change how it does it? There is a serious distinction between these two efforts. Changing what an organization does, i.e., its products or services, requires a different effort than changing how it does what it does, i.e., its processes. By trying to change an organization's products or services, it will probably also need to change its processes – but the opposite is not necessarily true. Changing what an organization does is not as painful to an organizational population as changing the way in which it does what it does.

According to Everett Rogers in his book *Diffusion of Innovation*, to implement an innovation (change) in any population, it requires an initial buy-in level of about 30 per cent. Once this level has been attained, the change effort will continue throughout the population group, becoming relatively unstoppable. This theory, which has been validated by the research Rogers put forth, applies to organizational populations as well. Some of the innovation efforts we have seen in recent years include the use of personal computers, the Internet and cellular phones. One of the reasons that Rogers' theory works can be seen in a causal loop diagram (see Figure 8).

Clearly, in the case of a business organization, the Rogers rule of obtaining the commitment of only 30 per cent of a given population to enable change to take place can depend a lot on who is in the 30 per cent. Whereas some people in management might assume that the 30 per cent number means 30 per cent of the managers, the reality is that what (or whom) you are looking for is people who are *key influencers* in the organization. Yes, senior decision-makers need to be onboard, as well as union leadership (if your organization is unionized), but by finding out who the people are that other employees look to for guidance, support, and information, you can find the 30 per cent you need. Quite often, key influencers are employees who have longevity in an organization – they have been there a long time, and have seen it all and know what makes sense and what doesn't. This group also has the advantage of being the ones who have experienced other initiatives and therefore, probably have recognized some of the pitfalls that were inherent in them. Yes, *senior* employees may also be some of the people who will want to resist change the most. They have been in the company a long time and might be tired of all the changes they have seen. But for this reason alone, it is just good thinking to try to get these people onboard first. If you can reach the 30 per cent that Rogers has targeted, your work in enabling change will be far easier.

The loop structure in Figure 8 can help us understand what is behind the diffusion theory, and points up a key leverage area to ensure a positive diffusion process. In the structure, as the organizational population understands the need for change, they can begin to believe in it. This increases their level of buy-in, which increases positive word of mouth, which in turn increases the visibility of the benefits of the change. This, in turn, increases the level of understanding of the need to change. This dynamic is reinforcing in nature, and the only thing that will change the effects of it is the number of people that the change will impact. The leverage area is found in the variable, '*understanding the need to change*'. Without an understanding of why an organizational population should accept a change effort, the effectiveness of that effort will be relatively doomed.

To help increase the understanding of the rationale behind a change effort, it is important to apply a rule of '*make the rationale behind the change concrete and often*'. This rule refers to several things.

First, by making the rationale 'concrete', management can begin to set the stage for a clear understanding of why the change will occur. This does not mean vague communications about the change efforts, or even worse, no communications at all. This can be devastating to an organizational population, and can begin or reinforce a belief that management is not telling the truth.

By making the rationale for change explicit, it will diffuse the informal communications network that, in many cases, disseminates incorrect information and rumour. Both incorrect information and rumour have a tendency to deflate an organizational climate. By making the rationale behind change explicit, however, many of the potential questions that might be raised at the water cooler or the coffee machine will be answered, thus, removing the fear of 'not knowing'. By making the rationale for change often, the potential to 'out run' the rumour mill will increase. This can be critical in an organizational environment in which the population may distrust or believe that management has something to hide.

Examples of the impact of not making a rationale for change concrete and often abound.

Example 1: An organization that was trying to implement a technology-based solution to help deal with a series of acquisitions. During the implementation process, there was quite a bit of confusion as to what was going to change, how it would impact the personnel, how long the implementation would take, or who it would impact. During this time of building concern and organizational chaos, the CEO of the organization was dismissed. The employees of the company read about this additional change in their local newspaper. Needless to say, this did not provide many assurances that the organization was stable and would be able to effectively implement the technology-based solution.

Example 2: An organization that was trying to implement a decentralization of a division. In this example, the initial announcement of the reorganization plan followed the 'rumour-mill' news dissemination by several weeks. As the plans began to come out of the executive offices, it came out in bits and pieces, usually just enough to try to diffuse the already present beliefs that were floating around the division. As the process moved forward, even the divisional managers were given information in small news bites. The overall plan didn't surface until the reorganization process had been moving for several months, and by that time, the motivation behind the plan was heavily discounted due to the poor level of trust in the division of the senior management.

Example 3: A large service organization had a training process for all of its employees that needed to be upgraded. The major problem here was the process of allotting funds for training. In the past, the organization culture included the belief that training was of utmost importance, and that the company provided training opportunities for all levels of employees. The process was one in which a department manager would meet with his or her employees and select an educational path for the employee. This was followed by formal written approval of the training request that was forwarded to the senior management manager for final approval. Due to the services provided by the organization, some departments were heavily involved in technology implementation, and personnel in those departments always had their training plans approved. But in most other cases, senior management did not approve training plans. To change this process, the overall approval was given to the departmental managers, and the change was made visible through meetings and personal visits by the training coordinator.

Example 4: A large healthcare provider was about to undergo negotiations with its unionized personnel. To ensure that the management was prepared to enter the negotiations with a systemic view of the various negotiation outcomes, the organization commissioned the development of a systems dynamics simulation model. The purpose of the simulation model was to 'test' the assumptions and theories of various negotiating strategies prior to them being 'put on the table'. Due to the need for buy-in to this process, the consultants charged with the development of the simulation began to make the simulation development process 'concrete early and often'.

As organizations begin to undergo change initiatives, on any level, one of the key drivers of their success is the ability of the organizational population to be able to see and understand the change, the methodology that will implement the change, and the rationale for the change.

Without these elements, a change process will become largely ineffective, with the only option for implementing it being a hard-core, militaristic approach. In light of the shift in management philosophies that has been seen in the past decade, the effect of this would be demise in the organizational culture and climate, resulting over time in devastating impacts on the organization as a whole.

Having said all this, it is important to remember that one of the reasons that change can be so difficult in an organizational environment is that there really are only four types of people in an organization: those who 'get it' and are supportive (these people usually are not a problem); those who don't understand the what

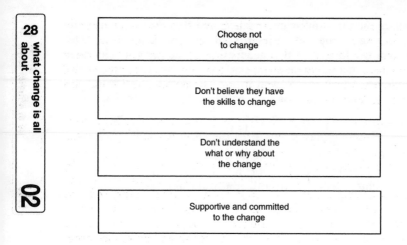

Choose not
to change

Don't believe they have
the skills to change

Don't understand the
what or why about
the change

Supportive and committed
to the change

Figure 9

and why of change; those who believe that they don't have the right skills to be able to change effectively; and those who just don't want to change (see Figure 9).

The group that doesn't understand can be helped through communications – clear, concise, open and complete – about what the organization needs to do, why it needs to do it, and how it will happen. The group that believes they don't have the skills to make the changes can be supported through training – again, clear, concise, open and complete. It is unreasonable to expect that managers or employees will be able to do what is needed if they don't have the skills to do it. And the group that is resistant? If they do understand, and they do have appropriate skills, then perhaps they need to have the opportunity to work for a different company. I have never been too keen to see people sacked for not changing unless you are sure they just don't want to work with you. Your company, your call.

Avoiding inappropriate addiction

Okay, so let's make a few assumptions – albeit big assumptions, but assumptions none the less. Let's assume your organizational population understands why the organization needs to change; they understand what needs to change; there is an environment that is conducive for change; and the managers and employees are up for the challenge. And let's say that they have actually developed a taste for change. How do you keep them from becoming addicted to change? In short, how do you keep them from focusing solely on change efforts and neglecting the actual mission work of the organization? The answer, as I hope you assume, is not an easy one.

Organizational change efforts that are ongoing in today's business world can play havoc with the current vogue of disseminating power throughout organizations. As many organizations try to bring more people into the corporate decision process, the constant movement of people in and out of organizations due to reorganization efforts can result in relative chaos, reduced options for accountability, lack of a cohesive collective organizational vision, and consequently, reduced organizational effectiveness – in short, these dynamics can and do reduce organizational performance potential. This is in part, due to senior decision-makers becoming addicted to the dynamics of change as well as hiding the potential destructive nature of ongoing change.

Two of the most often heard frustrations in organizations today are that performance is not what it should be, and the belief that change seems to be becoming constant. The change being talked about is organizational change, or in today's semantics, corporate reorganization. Reorganization itself has become a service industry, a focus for authors, and so entrenched in our culture; we tend to expect that our organizations will be reorganized over and over again. The performance that is being talked about is organizational performance. Period. It is the seeming inability of an organization to realize its potential over time. It is the fact that an organization cannot hit its target goals. It is that an organizational population seems to be 'off-track' and unable to focus on what is truly important. When these two frustrations 'boil over', usually what happens is the company begins to go through a reorganization process.

The intent of most reorganizations is to help the subject organization become more effective – to achieve higher performance levels. However, the evidence that we have seen is that long-term increases in effectiveness are minimal. This can be due to either the lack of sufficient time to measure results, or the short-term focus of the efforts. What is becoming apparent is the level of stress among the people affected by the change is increasing. An appropriate question might be, why then does it seem that many senior managers are becoming addicted to constant organizational change?

To explore this question, there are two things to consider – reality and what we believe that reality might be. In any organization, it is the perceptions that tend to 'curve' the actual reality. Hence, there are many reasons to implement, or try to implement a reorganization plan, based both on reality, and our sense of what we think reality is. These real or perceived reasons include an organization's inability to compete in the marketplace (real and perceived), the level of organizational effectiveness (real and perceived), the organizational ability to obtain the resources it believes it needs to exist (real and perceived), the organization's ability to plan strategically (real and perceived). These are all indicators of an organization's inability to perform at the level it needs to. In all these situations, the key element is the organization's 'perception' of itself. There is a connective relationship between an organization's perception of itself and its ability to understand its current reality. Most senior managers, the people who theoretically have overall organizational responsibility, appear to believe that they have a better view of this relationship than the rest of the organizational population.

As an organization's perceptions of itself drift from its reality, several dynamics begin to take place. These dynamics can be characterized by the mental models that become acted out by the employees of the organization. Mental models are the beliefs and assumptions that people hold about how their world actually works. Everyone has mental models – we have mental models about people, about situations, about relationships, and about how organizations should function. Simply having mental models is not bad; in reality, they form the foundation for organizational culture. What can become a problem, however, is when mental models differ largely from the reality of a situation. A good example is organizational complexity. We have found in our work that in most organizations, the level of perceived complexity (a mental model) is far greater than the real level of organizational complexity. When there is a variance like this, it can cause a severe decline in the ability of people to perform well, most often, because they think that the complexity level will inhibit their ability to perform. Examining individual and collective mental models can offer guidance as to what interventions are needed to ensure that the employees of an organization 'can' perform to the levels that are needed. The mental models that are important to examine include: 'we will never be effective if we keep changing', 'how can we increase accountability with constant change', 'are we still headed in the same direction as we were', and, 'how can we perform better when all we do is keep changing?'

1 We will never be effective if we keep changing.

This mental model can result in a diminished ability on the part of the employees to work as effectively as they can. This dynamic is not unusual. Until the late 1950s, it was a common belief that man could not run a mile in less than four minutes. This belief was reinforced by the fact no one had done so. When Roger Bannister broke the four-minute barrier, suddenly others began to run a mile in less than four minutes – *the belief that it could not be done was broken by the evidence that it could be done.* Through an example of a successful attempt, more success could be achieved.

In organizations, if we begin to believe that we will not be able to be effective due to ongoing reorganization efforts, the end result will be reduced effectiveness. Without appropriate benchmarks of success that can be quantified and qualified, people will feel that they are being put in a vicious circle of increased chaos. Effectiveness is a function of knowing where the organization is going, how it is to get there, and what part we all play in that movement. As the addiction to ongoing change increases, the potential for organizational effectiveness will decrease.

2 How can we increase accountability with constant change?

Accountability in organizations is usually defined as being evaluated on what we do and how well we do it. In an organization that is undergoing constant, ongoing change, it can be difficult to know what to do, and therefore, how to do it. Additionally, as organizations move their employees from division to division or shuffle old employees out and new ones in, the ability to know who is to do what is diminished. As we move people from one area to another while effectiveness efforts are underway, they will have a tendency to fall back into old ways of doing business – no rewards for effectiveness will lead to reduce effectiveness activity. Addiction to organizational change as a way to do business will decrease the potential for accountability in the organization.

3 Are we still headed in the same direction we were?

An ongoing problem in many organizations is the loss of organizational 'history'. It is the history, or organizational memory that can keep an organization from reliving many of the mistakes that organizations face over and over again. When the organization loses much of its capacity for retaining the history of the organization, it is not only doomed to relive the same mistakes over again, it can find itself being pulled and driven by both internal and external political influences. These influences have a tendency over time to change the stated direction or vision of the organization in a de facto manner. The organizational vision may remain constant, but the actions that the organization takes are in opposition to the stated vision, i.e., they are congruent with the organizational influences but not with the organizational collective knowledge. The addiction to change will decrease the ability to see and understand the long-term vision for an organization.

4   How can we perform better when all we do is keep changing?
This mental model is the most frightening, for it can create an environment in which non-performance becomes acceptable behaviour. This, of course, can be extremely destructive for it creeps through an organization with alarming speed – management is not able to hit targets, so the targets are adjusted. The new targets, in this type of environment are not met, so they are adjusted again, and again, and again. Eventually, performance is mediocre at best, and the end result is a company that will never realize its potential.

A result of these mental models and the actions they stimulate can be a belief on the part of senior management that the employees of an organization are not competent, nor have the capacity to help move an organization forward, resulting in less effectiveness over time.

This result will increase the addiction to constant organizational change. Addiction to re-organizational change causes increased evidence of these mental models and their subsequent actions, leading to more organizational change.

The outcome can be a belief that the senior management of an organization is literally leading the change for the sake of keeping enough fluidity to reinforce their position as the only ones who can lead the organization. By once again using diagrams that explain cause and effect relationships, the dynamics of ongoing change are relatively easy to see. The driver to change is usually a belief on the part of senior management that the organization is not as effective as it should be. The relationship between the problem symptom and the remedy is seen in Figure 10.

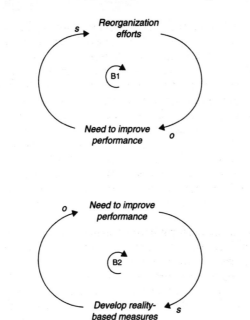

Figure 10

Figure 11

In this model, the less effective an organization appears to be the more senior management uses reorganization as a technique to remedy the situation. As the model shows, as the re-organizational efforts increase, the organization should increase performance, and, therefore, the less the organization should need to reorganize. Unfortunately, there is strong reason to believe that simple reorganization is a 'quick-fix' remedy, and its effects may not last over time. Another option to increase organizational performance is shown in Figure 11.

In this diagram, a long-term solution to a gap in the desired level of organizational performance and the current reality is the development of measures of effectiveness, i.e., performance, that are based in reality. This is a key point. If measures of effectiveness are simply pulled from the air, their potential will be nil. Developing measures of effectiveness, and holding the organization accountable for their achievement, will have the tendency to act as a long-term fundamental solution, not simply another quick fix.

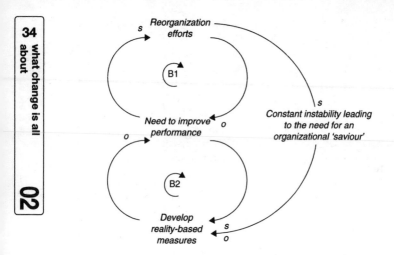

Figure 12

When both of these options for increasing organizational effectiveness are plotted together, the addiction dynamic becomes apparent (see Figure 12). The more senior management opts for reorganization as a method for increasing effectiveness (a short-term quick fix), the less stable the organization will be. This lack of stability can lead to the belief on the part of senior management that the organizational population is not capable of becoming more effective, and this will lead to a reinforcement of the belief of the need for someone who can 'save' the organization. The saviour of choice of senior management is, of course, senior management. If this dynamic falls into place, there would be no reason to implement reality-based measures, for the mental model in play is that the staff competency level is low and, therefore, not worth measuring. This can and will have a major impact on organizational accountability. Having no way to actively measure effectiveness, the organization falls back into reorganization as the technique of choice for increasing effectiveness, again providing reinforcement for the addictive behaviours of senior management.

As the addiction to organizational change grows, the mental models of the people affected by the changes tend to solidify. They include:

- It doesn't do any good to try to put forth an extra effort.
- Lack of knowledge is the real key to the problem.

- Constant change inhibits the potential for reorganization efforts to improve performance.
- We are just reliving 'quick-fix' actions of the past.
- Political influences are driving the change process.
- Chaos never allows real accountability to be evaluated.
- It is easier to blame than to learn.
- Pitting people against each other through blame eliminates putting forth extra effort.
- Questioning change efforts is extremely risky professionally, and can result in either public humiliation, the appearance of not being on the 'team', or possible termination.

The addictive dynamics of ongoing organizational change can result in several things. All will have a long-term detrimental impact on the organization and its potential over time. First, constant ongoing change creates a situation in which people rarely stay in a department or division long enough for any change efforts to take effect. This results in the loss of organizational history, which in turn leads to reliving organizational mistakes. Without the ability to 'remember' the organizational past, corporations and institutions will make costly avoidable mistakes.

Second, constant organizational change sets up the belief that few in the organization have knowledge as to what the next change will be, nor what the overall plan for change will be. Without a collective understanding of the 'big picture', it becomes more difficult to expect that the organizational population will be able to work collectively to help move the organization forward to achieve its goals and vision and, consequently, improve organizational performance.

Third, in conjunction with the previous characteristic, constant organizational change helps reinforce the organizational power structure – the same power structure that put the organization in the situation it is in. This is due to the lack of understanding or knowledge as to the overall change direction and plan. Consequently, there is the belief that some organizational power structures keep stirring the organizational pot to retain organizational control.

Fourth, constant organizational change leads to the ability of external forces to exert political pressure on senior management that can lead to knee-jerk reactions that are not in the best interests of the long-term future of the organization, its employees, and stakeholders.

part 2

stories from the office

03 how decisions impact change

In this chapter you will learn:

- how to avoid the negative impacts of quick-fix solutions
- how to make the best choices for the situation
- how to avoid recurring problems
- how to lead more effectively

The decisions we make, and more importantly, why we make them can have a major impact on our organization's ability to accept and survive change. Too often, little thought about the impact of decisions is put forth, even though, it is the decisions we make that cause employees to react the way that they do, and in the case of change, this reaction can often be negative.

The quick fix is still alive and well

Why quick-fix solutions can lead to organizational crises

In business, there has been an ongoing dynamic that says that in many organizations, managers and employees default their responsibilities to someone else. In most cases, this person is the CEO, who takes on the implicit role of organizational saviour. The dynamic is known as '*saviour as hero*' and one of the reasons this dynamic is present in organizations is because there is a belief that this is the only way to avoid crises. But according to Jim Collins (author of *Good to Great*), this dynamic seems to be shifting.

Collins and his research group have done a project that, '*challenges the assumption that transforming companies from good to great requires larger-than-life-leaders. The leaders that came out on top in Collins' five-year study were relatively unknown outside their industries. The findings appear to signal a shift of emphasis away from the hero to the anti-hero.*' I think that this view is missing the point, and even more importantly, it avoids the real issue.

Collins' premise is that current leaders who have demonstrated high competence have not come from the same industries in which they are currently working. Okay, but all that means is that, whilst organizations are still looking for heroes to save them, there seems to be a growing mental model that we need to look elsewhere for them than our own business or industry.

The implications are a bit frightening. If Collins is right, this could lead one to the conclusion that for whatever reason, organizations are finding it easier to look outside for fresh thinking than it would be to invest in bringing along some same-industry people by giving them the requisite skills to lead. Most certainly, if your organization continually finds itself mired in an environment where excellence seems to be only a word to be thrown around in marketing brochures, believing that by going outside you can save the day with someone who has an entirely different work experience you can accelerate the process of shifting from mediocre performance to exceptional performance. What does that say about the much touted commitments to organizational learning?

I am a big believer that being on the outside can provide a view that few people in an organization can see. It is the 'can't see the forest for the trees' metaphor in action. But I am also a big believer that the best way to avoid simply going from the frying pan to the fire is to ensure that your own organization has a solid plan to grow future leaders.

Again, whilst there are advantages to be had from bringing in 'outsiders', there can be some very serious negative unintended consequences from the decision.

1   Succession planning (whilst not exactly a high competence in many organizations now) may just end up with criteria that begins 'has worked in a different industry'. We all grow through experiences, and if existing managers do not gain the appropriate growth experiences, they will never be able to move up to senior leadership roles in organizations.

2   The belief that we can simply go outside to solve our problems instead of focusing on not having them occur will solidify further the mental models that all problems can be solved by just hiring a new person from the outside.

3   By looking outside for a new organizational saviour, companies run the risk of bringing in someone with 'unknown baggage'. Dealing with known commodities (and investing in improving them) is less costly than running the risk of new behaviours that may result in dissension, mistrust, and lack of commitment.

4   Looking outside can set up a vicious cycle – don't like who we have? Go outside and hire someone new; and if you don't like that one, go further outside and hire another new one; and if you don't like that one, we can always look on the planet Pluto I guess. That should be far enough away to ensure success.

Organizations are still looking for 'saviours', and whilst Collins is saying that there is a serious shift from finding them inside an organization, the desire to have someone come in and save the day continues. When will our organizations wake up to find that there is a lot of talent on the company rolls now . . . we just need to nurture them so that in the future, we will have our future leaders without having to look that far away.

Unless organizations put more effort into helping existing managers and employees grow into more senior positions, we will continue to be locked into a frame of mind that says our own people are not good enough. And if this is the case, then why have them employed at all?

A shift from 'the hero to the anti-hero'? I don't think so. It is more like a shifting of placing our bets on one hero to another hero, with the additional curve that the new hero may not have a clue about what you do or how you do it. Apparently business still loves the quick fix as the be-all, end-all solution to fundamental problems, and because of this illusion that the quick fix is the best solution, crises are still a high potential, but now for a different reason.

Questions

- Does your organization work to grow its own new leaders, or does it instead seek out external candidates from other industries?
- Whilst an 'external' candidate may bring new perspectives to long-standing problems, what else might occur due to this type of hiring criteria?
- What happens to the morale of internal managers when they are passed over for someone who has no experience in the business (or industry)?

Where has all the talent gone?

How losing organizational talent can lead to ongoing crises

This question – *where has all our talent gone?* – has been around ever since the first organizational competitor came on the scene, and losing good talent can generate either a real or perceived crisis. After all, growing and sustaining a business takes people; smart, competent people; and the easiest place to find them is at your competitor. And although most companies are shrewd enough to have employees sign non-compete clauses into employment contracts, in many cases, these clauses rarely stand up in court.

The options left to organizational human resource people are – these are the people who usually are tasked with finding the hot talent – (1) when your people are poached, return the favour and go poach some replacements from another company; (2) contract with the best head-hunters around to find good people (but using a head-hunter is just a polite way of poaching); (3) or try to ensure that your best people don't decide to leave.

Whilst all three options are possible, option one just represents a management decision that is pretty well locked into reactive thinking, and that usually results in more talent leaving over time. Option two can be great, but it also can be an expensive option and often results in existing talent fleeing the organizational scene if the 'new guy' comes in to change everything. Option three however, represents management decision-making that usually focuses on the long term, which over time makes tremendous sense. Remember, whilst the question in the heading is *'where has all the talent gone?'* the real question is, *'why would they leave?'*

Option three can be expensive, and I don't mean that the right way to keep talent is to just saturate them with high salaries. Option three can be expensive in *effort* . . . but the pay off is well worth it.

Most employee satisfaction studies have shown that whilst money is a great thing to have, most employees cite organizational climate as a principal reason that influences a decision to stay or go. So if you are tired trying options one or two, here is what you need to consider if you want to make option three viable.

1 Do your employees feel that their efforts make a difference?
2 Do your employees feel that they can contribute to the overall organizational direction planning process?
3 Do your employees believe that the management team is competent to lead the organization into the future?
4 Is your employees' feedback valued by management?
5 Do they believe it is valued?
6 Is your organizational environment one in which employees feel like they are part of a large team achieving goals, or is the environment between departments (and employees) adversarial?
7 Do your employees believe what management tells them?
8 Are your employees committed to organizational goals and initiatives, or just compliant?

9 If you paid them more money, would they be more committed, or just be quiet?
10 How do you really know the answers to these questions?

Now here is the sad part. Organizational management teams I have spoken to over the past dozen years seem to fall into four groups regarding these questions: (A) we don't know the answers to these questions; (B) we assume we know the answers to these questions; (C) we actually have asked these questions and have data to back up our knowledge; (D) we don't think these questions are as important as getting the work done, so we won't take the time to ask them. And even sadder, the number of management teams that are in group C are in the distinct minority.

Groups A, B, and D represent 'not knowing'. Group A admittedly doesn't know; group B is just guessing, which means they really don't know; and group D is too busy fire-fighting to even take the time to find out. The only 'bad news' in business today is not knowing; not knowing where the company is going, not knowing what roadblocks to future success may be looming out there, not knowing what the competition might be able to do, not knowing what your customers actually want, and not knowing if your employees are committed to the strategy and the way to implement it.

And even if you can figure out what the future holds, or what your competition might do next, if your people aren't committed to what needs to be done, you are in trouble. And if they *really* aren't committed, they will probably leave, and then what will you do?

Questions

- Does your organization have a problem with talent retention?
- Is there data on how big a problem it is, or why it is occurring?
- Is there a plan to deal with the problem?
- Have any of the unintended consequences of implementing the plan been considered?

Choking on success?

What can happen when too much success too quickly can result in problems

When it comes to a crisis, there isn't too much greater than not having any business . . . or so we think. There are organizations out there that experience the symptoms of business crisis for the exact opposite reason – wild uncontrollable growth. And too much business that you are not prepared to handle can put you out of business just as quickly as having none at all.

If there is one thing that can kill a business besides lack of growth, it is growth that is too fast. Stelios Haji-Ioannou, the founder of easyJet has been quoted as saying: '*The mistake we made was we grew too rapidly.*' Stelios was referring to the stories about some of the business units in his easyGroup (easyCar, easyInternetcafé, and the other 'easy' ventures that he is involved with). Whilst easyJet is a well-recognized success, the statement by the founder does beg the question, '*is sustaining growth really that easy?*' Clearly not.

Companies grow because they have a solid, well-recognized brand; they have happy customers who spend money with them; they have their cost structure firmly under control; and their senior managers are able to keep their eye on the ball. When any one of these variables starts to slip, growth ceases and it sends the other variables into a tailspin. And when that happens, the potential for sustainable growth ceases. So in the case of Stelios, when he said that they 'grew too rapidly' – a symptom of the real problem – it was probably a reflection on the slippage of one or more of those variables.

The easyGroup is a classic example of what can occur from fast growth. Managers begin to believe that the success they have generated can be repeated again and again. They begin to believe that their decisions will always work out right. They begin to assume that whatever they touch will turn to gold (or shocking orange in some cases). And they begin to believe that the market will follow them. Well sometimes they might be right. But repeatability of success can only happen when managers make sound decisions; and to do this, they need to ensure that their thinking, influencing, achieving, and leading faculties are in alignment. And too often, they are not.

The same thing occurred with another discount airline, People's Express. People's Express began in the United States in the 1990s as *the* discount American airline, and in a short period of time, was experiencing unbelievable growth. It was the darling of investors, and its results were quoted on a regular basis in the business media as having a formula for success. And then one day, seemingly out of the blue, it filed for bankruptcy.

To avoid this from happening to your organization, there are several things that you can do. First, begin to believe that your previous success may not solely be because you are smart. Organizational success is complex, and just because you can 'see' success again, it doesn't mean that everyone in your organization will 'see' the same picture in the same way you do. Spend time with your team and talk through all the complexities of what you are trying to accomplish. By 'talking it through', I don't mean you tell them that the plan is to repeat what you did previously. I mean that you and your team will need to figure out all the potential scenarios that you might encounter on your hoped for journey to repeated success. I wasn't there when easyJet started, but do you believe that some of the scenarios the senior team talked about included the current price of fuel to run the planes? Do you believe that they talked about the potential for a 9/11 happening and air travel falling? Do you believe that they talked about everybody and his brother getting into the discount airline business? Wasn't there, don't know. After the demise of People's Express, its story became a case study for many business schools, and because of this, many of the reasons for its failure have surfaced. It was experiencing such success that apparently no one bothered to ensure that its infrastructure was appropriate for its growth pattern, and even worse, apparently no one in management really pondered what else might occur if it kept growing at the rate it was.

The lesson here is that the only way to be ready for any contingency that can muck up your plans is to know what 'might happen'. And when you know what 'might happen', you can then either build a contingency plan for it, or reject the whole idea for being too risky.

The next thing you can do is work to avoid getting ahead of yourself. When things are going well, we quite often begin to skip over decisions that can, over time, have a tremendous impact in the future. Things worth doing at all are worth doing well. Take your time. Be sure that you have crossed all your 'T's and dotted all your 'I's. The devil is in the detail, and just rushing ahead at speed can cause some decisions to be fraught with problems.

Make sure that you have the right team of people working with you. In many organizations, the team that is charged with plotting out the future is comprised of like-thinking people. Well, okay, you do need to have people who share the same vision. But at the same time, you need to ensure that you have a blend of people who are not afraid to raise the tough questions and to say 'no' if they think something will not work out the way you want it to. You might want to use some tool like Myers Briggs® or OPQ or Belbin® to get a grasp on what your team can bring to the decision-making process. Remember, the chances of success are severely lessened if people who are all intuitive thinkers or data-heads surround you. Success in decision-making comes through a blend of thinking and influencing types. A caution here of course – these tools are just that; tools. In order to really get something from them, you need to realize that they represent decision-making models and their use is just a way to surface insights into why we think and react the way we do. And your team needs to realize that as well, and not treat them as a cute exercise that will be over in a couple of hours.

People's Express is out of business and with other competitors in the US market, will not re-start. But will Stelios be able to re-visit the success he has seen in the past? Well time will tell. But in the words of Mr Einstein, the same kind of thinking that got us into a mess will not get us out of it. Regardless of how successful you have been in the past, you need to remember that repeatable, sustainable success just isn't that easy.

Questions

- Are your company's growth plans on target?
- Are you able to match the growth of infrastructure with sales or headcount or services?
- Is the topic of managing growth expectations and delivered growth a recurring topic at management meetings? Do these meetings include, 'what will we do if . . . ?' conversations?
- Are there contingency plans in place for low growth or growth that exceeds plans and expectations?

Choices, bloody choices

Why not understanding available options can trap decision-makers

Here is the challenge that many organizations are faced with today: Do we, when faced with monetary problems, invest in our people, or save our money? Do we, as managers, follow the path that has been set by the company strategy, or do we deviate from the chosen path when some Board members try to influence us?

Do we fall into reactive thinking mode when the pressure is on, or do we stay the course? Whilst these questions are all important, the real question is, '*at what point, if at all, will our decision-making processes fail us?*'

Decision-making is all about making choices. Should we do this, or should we do that? Unfortunately, too often, our choices become a bit blurry when we lose sight of why our organizations even exist. Yes, we all believe that our choices will help us to make more profits, and that is the real bottom line of business. No profits, no business. But where we can get lost is knowing which things to do are the best things to do in any given situation? And which things to do will help us to satisfy the other parts of our business purpose?

A good test of the decision-making process is to validate decisions with the simple question: *will this decision choice help us to satisfy our organizational mission and our vision for the future better than another choice?* If the answer is no, then it is probably the wrong choice. Sadly, I have seen many examples of what can happen when this test is not applied.

The criteria, other than the organizational mission and vision, should include the values your company holds:

- Do your decisions support company values?
- Do your choices match up with all the rhetoric that senior management keeps putting out?
- Will your choices support the ongoing growth in learning of your employees?
- Will your choices make sense to your customers, suppliers, and employees?
- And do our choices represent proactive, rational approaches to challenges and problems, or do they represent reactions to problems that were not anticipated?

Another way to look at the decision-making process is to examine several key issues:

- Does your organization have competent people in key decision areas?
- Does your organization reinvest in its people?
- Does your organization seem to take longer than it should when accomplishing the goals set forth for initiatives?
- Do the managers and employees believe that the people leading the organization are the right people for the environment the organization is in?

Now it would be nice to be able to provide appropriate answers to these (and other) questions relating to making choices, but the reality is that in business, *there is no guaranteed right answer that applies in every situation*. And it is this fact that perhaps makes decision-making so interesting.

Good decision-makers often say that making choices in business is a combination of using hard data, and having a feeling for what to do. That combination might be true, but without having some basis to guide the decision itself, making choices in business is really not too much different than knowing which numbers will be called in a Lotto draw. The lesson is clear – make sure your decision choices make sense before you are forced to regret them.

Questions

- Is there a decision-making process in your organization? Do managers and employees know about it? Do they use it?
- Are the decisions tested before they are implemented?
- What happens if a decision appears to be inappropriate after the fact?
- How much time is spent dealing with poor decisions?

When is fast, fast enough?

Understanding the risks of making decisions too slowly, or too quickly

Whilst talking to a CEO about the concepts of change and crisis, two very interesting things arose, both of them relating to how change can lead to crisis (or so he thought). They were, '*I realize we need to speed up our company's decision-making, but how can we avoid having to revise 9 out of 10 decisions because we missed something?*' The second was, '*why is it that it appears that the dot-com bomb is sufficiently far enough away that many managers have stopped being worried?*' Whilst the questions are different, the real underlying issues are the same – *how to apply experience to our decision-making processes*.

The current situation in most organizations is clear: decisions need to be made with increasing speed due to competitive, regulatory, and other real and perceived pressures. And sadly, there is growing evidence that organizations are prepared to sacrifice logic and accuracy to achieve quick decisions.

If we believe the rationale behind the pressure for faster decisions (*less time to make a decision means less money spent whilst making it*), then doesn't it stand to reason that any time spent 'fixing' a poor decision is total waste? The waste is magnified when it becomes apparent, as it often does, that the same decision was tried before, and generated the same lame results. What folly is this?

A good friend of mine at Microsoft told me that his cautionary 'rule of thumb' about compressing the amount of time it takes to make decisions was, '*speed is everything, but that is how high-speed crashes occur*'. Well said.

It is clear that many managers need to get their heads around the fine line between 'fast' decision-making, and 'good' decision-making. Interestingly, you can have both. But to do so, it is important to be conscious of three things. First, it is ludicrous to expect that decisions should be delayed until all the potential downsides can be sorted out. I don't know of a single successful manager who waits until 100 per cent is 'right'. Most successful managers go with 70–80 per cent sorted. The key is to make sure which bits are sorted before going ahead. This leads to the second thing to understand.

It is crucial for fast, but sound decision-making, to have an understanding of what else might happen if you implement the decision. Understanding the 'what else might happen' question is a demonstration of sound systemic thinking, and is a good indicator of the competence of the decision-maker.

Third, avoiding delays in making decisions is something that all organizations should be trying to do. And whilst some organizations believe that they still have the luxury of time, the reality is that they don't.

The ability to make decisions – that is, effective decisions that achieve what needs to be achieved – is a key indicator of whether or not an organization will be able to achieve its goals. To do so, the decision-makers need to be able to recognize what is important, and what isn't. They need to sort through which decisions need to be made first. They need to be able to distinguish the difference between crucially important to help an organization satisfy its mission, and just the cool and sexy things that are really just distractions. And they need to do all the above without faffing about or causing even more problems than they had before.

If they don't, their organizations (and their people) will never be able to realize their individual and collective potential. And at the end of the day, that is how organizations make money. Period.

Questions

- In your organization, is there pressure to 'get things done quickly?'
- What are some of the unintended consequences of this?
- Are mistakes being made by rushing? What is the cost of these mistakes?
- What can be done to alleviate the pressure, whilst at the same time, ensure that internal and external needs are met on time, and in full?

Wicked, wicked problems

How we cause many of the crises we suffer from

Too often, organizations trying to survive through change efforts end up having what we call 'wicked, wicked problems'. In an organizational context, 'wicked problems' are defined as those *'where behavioural complexity is high; and where different groups of key decision-makers hold different assumptions, values, and beliefs which are in opposition to each other'*. Apparently, there are many organizations out there that suffer from some form of this malady.

Example 1: I know of several extremely large organizations (all from different business sectors) that have made investments in how to learn from the past. They had contracted with some pretty competent researchers who had developed a way to help organizations learn how to leverage good decisions, and avoid making bad decisions again. After the researchers had compiled some serious volumes of work, a report was presented to the senior team of one of the organizations. Whilst at the time, everyone vowed to take this information and use it to avoid the pitfalls of the past, over time, nothing really changed.

Example 2: The CEO of an SME was concerned that his employees weren't able to keep up with the changing world his company had found itself in, and decided to bring in a hard-core change programme. The other three senior guys were extremely supportive of this, as they recognized that if the company didn't change the *way* in which their people did their work, the company would never be able to resume its previously spectacular growth pattern. The programme was very well received, but after a two-year period, everything was as it had been previously.

Example 3: The head of a mid-sized organization was sacked and a new person was brought in to fix all the existing problems, and in the process, renew the organization. Over several years, he tightened up the processes and procedures, got rid of the incompetent managers that thought they were safely lodged in lifetime employment, and managed to turn the organization's financial picture around. He had worked extremely hard to put in place a structure that would last over time, but shortly after he retired, the company began to slowly revert back to its previously lacklustre performance pattern.

In all of these examples there are several common threads.

First, learning to do things differently is a choice. You can have someone harangue you that there is a better way, but unless you decide to believe what you are told, you will not learn how to apply the 'better way'. This is complicated by the fact that, if you don't believe it yourself, the chances that you will become a disciple of the 'better way' are slim to not at all. Consequently, learning is not transferred to others, and nothing ever changes. In the first example, the ability to learn from the past was implicitly blocked by managers who, without malice, decided that all this new information wasn't as important as hitting the numbers now. And because their company was, due to events beyond their control, inundated with the cash that was rolling in so fast, there was no sense of urgency to apply the learning.

Second, whiplash-like change efforts can numb an organization. It was well understood by employees that the senior team of the SME had a pattern of behaviour of getting all fired up about something new, but their ability to wait for results over time was measured in nano-seconds. They would drag the organization from one super hot initiative that would change their world to the next; often not even giving time for the initiatives to take hold, and this sent the signal that if the managers and employees would just hold their breath for a bit, something new would come along anyway.

Third, mental models of managers and employees, which are compiled over years, cannot be changed quickly. We all build our mental models based on experiences and observations, and then use these mental models to guide our own decision-making processes. And whilst we may be told that there is a better way, as soon as there isn't any reason to change, many of us take the path of least resistance and revert to old ways and patterns of behaviour.

Whilst many organizational problems do appear to be wicked, the only real wicked problems that companies face are the inability to really ensure that management operates with one voice, with a coherent set of mental models, a consistent message, and a consistent vision for the future. If they aren't able (or willing) to operate in this manner, their ability to ensure that their company will be able to realize its potential will be about as good as you or I winning the lottery tonight. The question that these wicked, wicked problems generate should be, 'what can we do to avoid these problems from occurring in the first place?'

By looking at the real fundamental problems (not just the very visible symptoms of the problems that most organizations tend to fixate on), it is not that difficult to understand how to avoid them in the future.

In the first example – learning to do things differently is a choice – ensure that you communicate the fact that the managers do have a choice. There is no 'set' or 'right' answer to problems that arise, and clearly, although there might be a 'better way', it must be remembered that the current 'better way' at one time was just another new idea.

I spent some time working with a CEO who had, as his 'fixed' response to working out customer problems, to use the company's 'customer service process response' (CSPR). Whilst this process was pretty good, the very fact that customers were still coming to the company's management with problems meant that it wasn't the end-all, be-all. But when I asked the CEO why the company didn't explore other options for dealing with customer issues, the response was, 'this is the process we use'. Fair enough. But when I then asked if this was the only process they used, his response was something to the effect that, 'no, we used to have a different process but we stopped using it when I came up with the CSPR.' This was a real potential learning opportunity: in the past, they had a different process but when the CEO came up with a new one, they switched, but now were being told to keep what was 'working'. Very interesting is the fact that it wasn't working all the time. Because the CEO had a sense of ownership of the current process, he had effectively removed the willingness of the managers to even attempt a new solution. In this situation, there was no sense of choice being an option, and it took quite a while for the CEO to encourage his people to accept that there just might be a new, better way. And he did do this as soon as he made the conscious choice to believe it himself. Having the ability to choose is important; believing you have it is equally important.

In the second example – whiplash-like change efforts can numb an organization – both the explicit and implicit messages about the need for instant results had driven the management team to become restless and not allow for the benefits to materialize. And because of this behaviour, the employees realized that change programmes would rarely (if ever) reach completion, and, consequently, would not feel compelled to put in the effort that should have been required. This dynamic has occurred in many organizations, for many years.

In the latter part of the last century, many organizations attempted to implement programmes such as Total Quality Management (TQM). And whilst all the information about how to do this explained quite clearly that, due to the fact that managers and employees would be forced to learn how to do things differently, and consequently their performance will go down before it improved, many management teams dropped the programme efforts at or near to the low point of the performance dip, not having the patience to now reap the benefits of the soon-to-occur rise in performance. Instead, they simply moved on to the next big business performance improvement method.

It didn't take employees long to realize that this was occurring, and many of the employees to grasp that the efforts would not be realized due to management's decisions (and impatience), and consequently, the beliefs that some of these business improvement programmes wouldn't work to begin with became self-fulfilling prophecies.

The third example – mental models accumulated over time cannot be modified easily – tells the real story about an ability or inability to accept change. And if you examine the first two examples closely, it is clear that this example explains both of them even more clearly. If managers *believe* that they do not have choice – regardless of what they have been told – they will not act as if they do. If managers and employees *believe* that senior decision-makers do not have the patience to wait for better results, they will act accordingly and not worry about doing everything they can to achieve the improved results.

It is pretty commonly held that most of us make decisions based on our beliefs. Peter Senge, author of *The Fifth Discipline*, once said, '*do we believe what we see or do we see what we believe?*' I think that Peter is right – we don't just believe what we see; we tend to see what we believe, especially in business. People have the ability to take their beliefs and craft them into truths about what an organization is doing, for what reasons, and if it even makes sense. And then, it can be these mental models that cause us to filter out the true reality of a given situation.

A good example of how this happens was recently given to me by a retired CEO from Australia. Whilst talking about how managers make decisions, Kelvin Hack asked me, '*if you are hovering over Los Angeles California in a helicopter, and wanted to travel to Reno Nevada, which direction would you go?*' He also asked me '*what would be the first country I would encounter if I was in Detroit Michigan and went directly south?*' Having spent many years in the US, I felt quite confident that I knew the answers, only to be surprised that my answers were not correct.* Kelvin's questions caused me to reflect on how often we make decisions based on what we believe without taking the time to find out if what we believe has any semblance to the reality of the situation.

Humans live in one of those 'good news–bad news' environments. We possess the capacity to make decisions based on accumulated knowledge – that is the good news. The bad news is that quite often, our accumulated knowledge is stilted by our beliefs and assumptions, and in many cases, it is these beliefs and assumptions that cause us to make decisions that in hindsight look quite daft. This dynamic is a plague in the world of business.

I know of several CEOs and MDs who are extremely bright guys, but too often, they are so caught up in their own beliefs that are quite removed from the reality of a specific situation that the decisions they make get them into trouble over time. For example, I recently met an MD who really believed that his workforce was aligned and thought he was the best person to lead the company into the future. I asked how he knew this, and he told me that he had asked some of his direct reports and they all told him that he was. Okay, fair enough, but when I asked him

* The correct answers to Kelvin's questions are 'Northwest' and 'Canada'.

if he was confident that their answers reflected the reality of the environment, his reply was that it was, and if I didn't believe it, I could ask the employees myself. So I did, and what I found was startling. Whilst all of the MD's direct reports did confirm the information, front-line workers (the ones who actually do the real work of the company) had a different view.

The level of alignment (support for senior management decisions) was perilously low. Almost 25 per cent of the employees I spoke with said that it didn't make a difference who was the MD – the company would just keep ticking along, and over 50 per cent said that the MD was 'out of touch' or 'less than qualified' to lead. (*I have cleaned up their actual responses quite a bit.*) When I reported this to the MD, his two main concerns were '*who said that?*' and '*they don't know what they are talking about*'. His beliefs – reinforced by information that was provided to him by people who were less-than-objective – didn't allow him to even consider the possibility that his view might be incorrect. And because of this, he was making decisions about employees that were distorted.

Too often, managers find themselves trapped into accepting their existing mental models about situations because they are convinced that their mental models reflect reality. In short, they only 'see' what they have already deemed to be what they should be looking for. And this can result in devastating problems over time – problems about what goals are worth striving for; problems about what it will take to achieve the goals; problems about what else might happen as activities designed to achieve goals are implemented; and problems about how to sustain the gains achieved.

If managers wish to become more effective at what they do, they need to be willing to examine their own beliefs and assumptions, and if they are shown to be less than accurate, change them. If not, they risk making decisions that may plague them long into the future. Managers need to know that they have choices, and that exploring what those choices are is a good thing. Managers and employees need to know that change efforts may not generate instant improvements, and that patience may be a behaviour that they need to work on.

Recently, whilst talking to a good friend, the subject of 'divining' came up – you know, using some mystical way to find something. But instead of talking about finding water in the desert, the question that was raised was, '*are companies flexible enough to survive through a change effort (without sacrificing the mission/vision)?'* The answer is, *'they can be'*.

Finding opportunity is a function of both understanding what you do, and what you *can* do. Too often, however, many key decision-makers become locked into a mental model that *'this is how we do change initiatives, because this is how we have always done them'*. A fair mental model, but it does reflect a rather myopic view of what it takes to be successful in today's business climate. In order to increase the potential for organizational success, it is important to view *'what you do'* from a different perspective.

Several years ago, I was working with someone who had a clear vision of what her organization should become in the future. Over a series of meetings, I kept pressing for reasons of why that vision was so important, and eventually was able to determine that the vision was important, because it *always had* been important. Not exactly the best reason to try to steer an organization in a certain direction I thought.

I asked the CEO what she would have if her company were able to achieve her vision, and her response was predictable. *'If we achieve our vision, we will be the best in our market'*. A good, but still myopic response. *'If you achieve your vision, will part of what you have be that your company will have realized its potential?'* I asked. *'I hope so'*, was all she could say. This, unfortunately, is just not good enough, especially in today's marketplace. The challenge she faced was not just realizing her company's vision, but to make sure that the vision wasn't too restrictive. A restrictive vision (or mission) is one of the biggest impediments to finding opportunities that can help an organization grow.

CEO-types (and other key decision-makers) need to begin to ask themselves a series of questions, and whilst these questions might be painful, they are critical.

1 What is the vision for the future of the organization?
2 Why is this vision so important?
3 If we attain the vision, what will we really have achieved?
4 What else will we have achieved?
5 Are there other ways we could achieve the same things?
6 Are the potential scenarios that our organization may encounter as we change going to help us or hinder our ability to achieve the vision?

7   How will we deal with these potential scenarios?
8   If opportunities arise along the way to change the way we
    deal with change, will we be flexible enough to take advan-
    tage of them?
9   How will it be able to do this?

Now whilst all the questions are important, it is the last two
questions that will really tell the story about whether or not the
organization will be flexible enough to take advantage of opportunities to realize its potential.

Organizations need to understand what their processes and
systems really do, and what their employees' capabilities really
are. In most cases, this information is currently not available,
largely because the answers are found in typical 'check-sheets' that
reside in a filing cabinet in someone's office – *we have this or that
system, we use these processes, and our people have these skills*.
Nice information to have, and it does look great in an annual
report, but with this type of thinking, it will be pretty difficult for
an organization to capture opportunities (or create them).

To really understand systems, processes, and capabilities, what
needs to be done is determine *'what else'* the systems *can* do,
'what else' the processes *can* do, and *'what else'* the employees'
capabilities are *able* to accomplish.

With this information, the perspective of what a company does,
and how it does it can change. And if the perspective can change,
the ability to seek out, and take advantage of, opportunities
increases dramatically.

The ability to be flexible can be a key differentiator for business
success, and like most things in business, being more flexible is a
choice.

Questions

• Does your organization suffer from ongoing, fundamental,
  recurring problems?
• What is being done to eliminate or reduce the number and frequency of them?
• Do management have an understanding of what the real
  causes are of these problems or do they view them in terms of
  problem symptoms?
• What could be done to expand their view on what causes the
  problems?

Leading by example

Understanding how others see our own behaviours

Michael Eisner, the fabled head of the Disney organization, recently gave an interview in which he said that he had '*shrugged off the turbulence that often accompanied his 21 years at the helm of the Mouse House, saying that it has always resulted from trying to improve the company*'. Sure Michael; we all try at times to rationalize our own behaviours, don't we?

Eisner, in his years at the helm of the company, had made quite a reputation for restoring some of the magic to the magic kingdom of Disney, but he also made quite a reputation for thriving on conflict. However, according to Eisner, the only time he '*had conflict was when someone was trying to compromise either our ethics or they were trying to compromise the quality of our products*'. Apparently this must have been happening seven days a week.

Being the head of an organization, regardless of size or sector, can be challenging; but this does not mean it must necessarily be full of turbulence. Reducing the amount of turbulence experienced by an organization should be a principal responsibility of leadership. Organizational turbulence leads to chaos and confusion; it leads to lack of motivation and commitment; and it leads to an adversarial organization that can't realize its potential. And in most cases, organizational turbulence is a direct result of the way the guy at the top leads.

One of the biggest problems in the senior offices of management teams is that, whilst the top guys are quick to criticize the behaviours of the mid-managers and employees, they often delude themselves into thinking that their own behaviours have not contributed to the situation. Being a manager, at any level, means it is necessary to look into a mirror and see what behaviours others see. But too often, what they see in the mirror is modified by a magically modified managerial perspective that only shows them what they want to see.

If a manager is really interested in becoming a better leader, there are some questions that he or she should ask whilst looking in the mirror.

1 Do I share my picture of what our organization can be in the future with my team and my employees? Is the picture I describe clear? How do I know?

2 Are my people supportive and committed to help achieve this vision? How do I know?

3 Do I ensure that my managers and employees have the skills they need to be able to help achieve this vision? How do I know?

4 Am I supportive and committed to ongoing training and creating learning opportunities for the employees to increase their skills? How do *they* know that?

5 Is my coaching and mentoring of my direct reports making a difference? Am I competent to be a coach?

6 Am I really open to honest feedback about the way I lead the organization? Do the employees know this?

7 Do my behaviours and decisions lead to more turbulence in the organization, or a reduction of it? How do I know that?

8 Do my peer managers and employees really believe that I am competent to lead this organization? How do I know?

9 What would I do if I thought that they didn't think so? How would that help?

10 What don't I know that I should know?

Being the head of an organization (or a department or business unit) requires an understanding of what is going on in the organization, and why. But being confrontational or using conflict to stimulate results is not the way to make things happen, nor is it the way to ensure that the organization will be able to realize its potential.

Bosses need to be stabilizing anchors for an organization, and to do this requires different behaviours about how managers and employees think, influence, achieve, and lead. And as stated before, these behaviours will only be learned and accepted by the employees and managers if they are seen being demonstrated by the bosses.

Tomorrow morning, when you get to work, you may want to look into a mirror and ask yourself, '*Am I doing all that I can to avoid organizational turbulence?*' And if your mirror says that you are, you may want to go out and buy a new mirror. We can always do better at what we do.

Questions

• Are the senior people in your organization leaders or managers? Are you a leader or a manager?

• Do you accomplish goals through motivation or by mandate?

- Are you happy with your demonstrated leadership behaviours? Are the people you work with happy with them?
- What could you do to be a better leader?

When teams go bad

How to avoid crises from occurring

Whilst working on this book, I received an email from a senior manager in a medium-sized global service provider. His letter brought forth a dilemma that extends far beyond his specific question.

The email said:

> Having an effective Board of Directors can be key to the success of an organization. Board members are supposed to act as advisers on all key decisions that impact an organization; they should be able to help keep a company on track; help management manage better; provide key counsel when counsel is needed; help use their individual and collective networks to cut through some of the red-tape that can delay progress; and, add credibility to what an organization is attempting to accomplish. All this is fine, but sometimes, after a Board member has been added to an existing group, you find that the new member is out of touch with the direction and purpose of the company, and/or, just doesn't add value to the decision-making process. And when this occurs, what do you do?
>
> The easy answer is that you sack him, but the reality is that sacking a Board member can lead to complications. This is not to say that a dysfunctional Board member should be kept on just because you don't want to go through any more pain. Like any other decision in business, the real question is how to avoid this problem from occurring. Again, what is the best thing to do?

Well, yes, sacking the less-than-effective Board member is a solution, but it is really just a solution that deals with the symptom of the problem and not the underlying causes; and because of this, the company is at risk of seeing the return of the problem very soon.

Hiring and retaining good people in an organization, regardless of position, involves a set of choices. In the case of hiring, some of the choices revolve around:

A Does he or she have the right technical skills to do the job?

B Does he or she have an appropriate level of interpersonal skills?

C Does he or she 'see' the same picture as the peer group regarding where the company is, where it is going, and how it will get there?

D What extra baggage does this person bring to the position? (Baggage can be both good and bad. Good baggage usually relates to previous job experiences where substantial learning has taken place; and bad baggage usually relates to less-than-effective interpersonal relational skills.)

The choices around A, B and C are relatively easy to determine, but the challenge is to find out about D. Unfortunately, resolving the questions around D usually end up with anecdotal information that can be less than accurate. However, there is a way to gain a sense of what extra baggage might be part of the potential hire. The way is to ask for a story.

Stories are very powerful ways to find out what causes people to react the way they do in certain situations. Quite a few years ago, I was involved in several key hiring decisions for one of the 'Big 5' consultancies. Whilst the company interviewers concentrated on the specific skills needed to fill the position (asking relatively banal questions about, 'when faced with this or that situation, how would you put together a response' and the like), when it was my turn to ask the interviewee questions, I responded with, 'can you tell us a story?'

The story I was looking for was any story that the interviewee had heard from the time he could remember hearing stories until the previous day. Any story. It really didn't make any difference what story he told, as long as it was a story that had stuck in his mind. The only real parameter was that he had to 'tell a story', which is different from responding in 'PowerPoint language', simply spitting out a series of verbal bullet points. There was a reason for my request.

I was looking to find out several things. First, could the candidate actually tell a story. People don't respond well to bullet points, and it has been well established that through stories, people can be highly motivated (or de-motivated). I wanted to find out if this person, being interviewed for a relatively senior role, would be able to motivate and lead others in the organization. Second, by listening to the story, it would be an opportunity to establish something that was important enough for the interviewee to keep the story in his mind for many years (in this example, the story was something he had learnt when he was in his mid-teens). People are able to recall things in their minds that are important to them, and without any previous notice of my question, his response would be either something he was making up on the spot, or a real story that had stuck with him.

After listening to the story, I then asked him why that story was important enough to remember. Here I was looking for a connection between the message of the story (all stories contain messages) and why he found it valuable enough to hold in his mind for such a long time. And lastly, I asked him how the story he told would help him in the new position.

In this hiring process, what we were trying to avoid was hiring someone who may have had brilliant technical skills, but would not be able to function well in a complex organizational structure that was undergoing constant change. The same holds true for the email example about the Board member who 'suddenly' appeared to be acting in a dysfunctional manner. The reality is that had the people who interviewed him looked deeper into what was important to him before he was made a Board member, they might have been able to see a potential disconnect, thus avoiding a hiring crisis at the Board level.

The email, however, explained that the person was already onboard and the question was what to do about the existing problem. Clearly, sacking the man was an option, and an option that most Boards might opt for. After all, a dysfunctional Board is not conducive to guiding a highly functional business. But simply getting rid of a 'problem' may result in a new and different problem arising. I have always found it better to first try to work through the problems and build a cohesive, highly effective team.

Quite often, people exhibit behaviours that may appear to be dysfunctional in a team environment because they either do not see how they fit into the team structure, or because their views on the direction and means to achieve it are at odds with the balance of the group.

In the example, the implication is that the other Board members had been working together for some time, and over that time, they were probably able to grow into a functioning decision-making body. But with the addition of a new member, the cohesiveness of the team could have been disturbed, resulting in a growing collective mental model that the problem was 'the new guy'. It very well might have been the new Board member who was so far out of step with the rest of the group. But the bigger question is, 'why?' Were his views in opposition to where the Board felt the company should go, or were they different regarding how it should get there? Not being in alignment with an organization's direction can be a serious problem at the Board level (or at any level in a company), but not having alignment regarding how to achieve the direction that has been set forth may simply mean that the new Board member had some other ideas of how to move forward. If this was the case, it was a simple case of the rest of the Board not finding value in exploring all avenues. This represents an unwillingness to even consider that there could be another way. This is the typical change problem – we talk about how important change is, but when we are faced with it ourselves, we find it too difficult.

Was the Board simply going through an evolutionary change itself, and desperately trying to hold on to the status quo of being an existing team? If so, it would imply that regardless of who was brought in, there would be a problem, and therefore, sacking him and hiring someone new would only result in the same problem in a few months.

A sound path to take at this juncture would be to structure a facilitated conversation at the Board level to determine what the real problem was. The key would be to employ the services of a trained facilitator who can function in a highly politically-charged environment (which most Board of Director's meetings are). Through the facilitation process, it should be clear if the problem is one of skills, beliefs and assumptions, or just a dislike for the new person. It is then, and only then, that a decision should be made as to what to do.

Questions

- In your organization, what are some of the criteria used in making hiring decisions?
- Do interviewers make an attempt to discover interviewee mental models about the organization, where it is going, and how it will get there?
- How do they do that (or why don't they do that)?
- How often does your organization resort to sacking people as the solution to apparent non-alignment problems?

Gaining commitment or getting compliance?

Making change easier to accept

If there is something that senior managers don't like to talk about, it is their ability (or inability) to get people onboard with their initiatives. This issue is hidden in a shadow of semantics, with the essence of the topic being, what exactly does 'onboard' mean?

The word onboard is a historical reference to getting people on a ship before a journey. But this is where the problem lies: are the people 'onboard' because they have been told that they need to be, or are they 'onboard' because they think that this journey is sound and worthwhile?

For many managers and employees, getting onboard with strategic initiatives, or other change initiatives, means that they are following the company line that was set forth by the lads in the top jobs. They do this because they are told that this is what needs to be done. But do they believe it? This is where the distinction between *compliance* and *commitment* lies.

If you get your people onboard because they have been told to be onboard – compliance – they will not put forth the efforts that you need from them. However, if you can get commitment to your strategic direction from them – they are onboard because they *want to be* onboard and *see the benefits* from moving in this direction – you will find that they will provide the fabled 110 per cent that will probably be needed if you are to be able to really achieve the strategic goals and targets.

Here is where the darkness is: how can senior management gain *commitment* from their managers and employees? Too often, the methods used to gain commitment can be summarized by the adjectives *weak*, *ineffective* and *demeaning*. No wonder companies rely on compliance to drive initiatives. This need not be the case.

Commitment to just about anything is put forth because people *want* it. They see the big picture; they see the benefits of it; they see how they fit into it; and they see how their efforts can contribute to its success.

Internal marketing efforts are good vehicles to put clarity around the first two items; what is the big picture, and what are its benefits? But internal marketing usually falls short on helping managers and employees see how they fit into the big picture, and fall even further short on helping them see how their efforts can make a difference. Yes, slick, four-colour brochures and a deluge of emails can attempt to address the questions, but the reality is that the people driving these efforts (senior management) need to get out of the office and start talking to, and listening to, their people.

Now if you are a senior manager of a company that has thousands of employees, this might seem a bit daunting. You don't need to listen and talk to everyone; but you do need to find out who the key influencers in your company are, and sit down with them. Being a key influencer has little to do with hierarchical status; but more to do with internal networking and respect.

Find out who some of the people in your organization, the managers and employees, look up to and listen to. Seek them out and talk with them, but even more importantly, *listen to them*. If you can understand their concerns about what you want to accomplish, there is a good chance that you can get them to see why it is so important, and how they can help make it real. The worst thing that can happen is that you will not be able to get them onboard, so listen closer to what they say; the best thing is that you just might learn something about how to do it better next time and avoid having to fight this battle over and over again.

Questions

- In your organization, is compliance enough, or do management strive to gain commitment to initiatives?
- Do they get it? How do they know?
- How much commitment is required to actually see a demonstrable change in the way business is done?
- Do you have that much?
- What could be done to gain it?

04

how our beliefs impact change

In this chapter you will learn:

- the impact of mental models on success
- how to help shift beliefs and perceptions
- how to avoid the traps of inappropriate self-belief
- how to know your options

Our personal and collective mental models have a considerable impact on how we accept change, as well as on how well we can deal with organizational crises. This can be even more complicated as crises are much like art: they are in the eye of the beholder.

Another shark in formaldehyde?

Why the impact of change is often lost due to employee perceptions

Too often, organizations under pressure to change suffer from additional dilemmas. Who in the organization is competent to lead the change effort? How do we ensure that all the effort really accomplishes something? How will we know when we are done? These are all fair questions, but unfortunately, there is no singular answer that is always correct to any of them. Instead they set up a new Damien Hirst-like question. Several years ago, the Tate museum in London shocked the world by exhibiting Hirst's latest work – a shark suspended in a box filled with formaldehyde. And in the art world, it stimulated the question, *'is it art?'* A similar question arises from most change programmes: *when is a change effort really creating a new environment and not simply as effective as rearranging the deck chairs on the Titanic?*

I once received a letter from a manager who was concerned that the people who were leading the change effort in his company were not really competent to do so. His question was *'how can I show them what they really need to do if they don't see it themselves?'* My experience is that you can't. About the only way to ensure that people decide to do something differently is to help them see the gap between what they do now, and what they need to do in the future. All the talking in the world about shifting behaviours will not carry an iota of weight as compared to managers and employees discovering the gap themselves. But, if you can help them see the gaps that might be present between where they want to go (and why), and where they are now; and what skills they need to have to drive change, and what skills they have now; the potential that they will want to have those gaps close is highly increased.

To see the gap between where you want to go and where you are, assemble a small group of managers and articulate *all* the dimensions of what the future organization they want (or need) are. This is an important point; *all* the dimensions means a picture that looks at more than just the financial aspects of the desired future. The reason for this is two-fold; first, the *numbers* are just outcomes of the newly changed organization. What you want to be able to see are the dimensions of the organization that will drive those outcomes. You should do this with more than one group – different managers have different perspectives, and it is always best to see if there is alignment in how the challenge is seen.

Second, if numbers are all that is important, just save your time and go out and buy a few hundred whips and force everyone to work harder until the numbers are achieved. This is lame, old thinking that is both not sustainable, and not workable anymore. The dimensions you are after are answered by questions like: What systems and processes will be needed in the future? What reward structures will be needed? What mental models will be required? What levels of alignment in thinking? What competencies will be needed? When you get some consensus as to this picture of the desired future, then identify what the *current* organizational dimensions are. Rest assured, there will be a gap, and in some organizations I have seen, the gap is rather intimidating. But because your competition is closing their gaps, you have to.

Next, sit down with the managers who will be charged with making the change programme successful and show them the outputs from the previous exercise, and then ask them what they are prepared to do differently *beginning tomorrow* to close the gaps. But if you really want this effort to succeed, ask them what they will do differently in four specific managerial competency areas: how they think, how they influence, how they achieve, and how they lead. After they have done this, they need to do a peer and subordinate review. Do their responses make sense? Will these new demonstrated behaviours in thinking, influencing, achieving and leading, be able to close the gaps between where the organization wants to be and where it is? Historically, when doing this review, managers discover, and come to the self-realization, that what they have done in the past will just not cut it in the future.

Yes, you may experience push-back or at very minimum, looks of bewilderment, but managers need to realize that the organization is the way it is because of the decisions that had been made up to that point in time, and *the way they acted those decisions out.* If the organization is to change, i.e., become a sustainably high-performing organization, then managers need to realize that the only way it will happen is if they do things differently.

All the memos from the home office; all the veiled threats from analysts; all the yelling and whinging from employees and customers alike will not change behaviours unless managers can see for themselves what needs to be done. And the only effective way for them to do this is to see it for themselves.

If your managers decide that they don't want to do this, or think that they are too busy or important to do this, then you may want to just ring up Damien Hirst and see if he can put them in formaldehyde too. Who knows, they might be more valuable then than they are now.

Questions

- How do you know what 'right' means in your organization?
- Is there any flexibility in the term 'right'?
- Do you believe that decision-makers in your organization think in binary terms (right or wrong) or systemic terms (what causes what)?
- How do you handle push-back for ideas?
- How could you handle it better?

Risk prevention, lesson 1

How to avoid some of the risks of not changing

Talking to a CEO recently, I was amazed at what I heard. He was trying to balance the conflicting budget demands from his company's public relations department and that of his legal department. His company, in the transportation sector, had recently experienced what he called a 'manifested risk' and the two departments were vying for extra funding to deal with the problem. The last time his company had a 'manifested risk', it had turned into a full-blown crisis, and he was not keen to have that occur again. Whilst his problem was a serious one, what concerned me was that he was asking the wrong question.

Instead of just trying to figure out the negative impacts of the problem, I encouraged him to think first of how to ever prevent this problem from occurring again. '*Sure,*' he said, '*of course we want to make sure the problem never occurs again, but if we don't get our heads around the current problem, we could be in serious legal problems due to possible liability.*' That was an obvious statement, but in most cases, when fire-fighting is the mode of thinking in an organization, management rarely gets

around to thinking in terms of developing fundamental solutions
to prevent problems.

This dynamic is known as shifting the burden: a management
culture that relies on fire-fighting as the way to deal with current
and future problems becomes addicted to the behaviour and this
addiction represents a reinforcing structure that usually results in
the decision-makers from instead opting out to prevent the problems from occurring. This behaviour in organizations is, in a
word, ludicrous. There have been enough studies that have
shown that preventing problems is less costly than trying to deal
with them when they occur that you would think by now that
preventive thinking would make more sense than fire-fighting,
but apparently, this is not the case.

And if the studies haven't shown management the best way, you
would think that the regulators would have. I can't think of any
mid-size to large company that doesn't have a health and safety
department. And most organizations believed that it is the
responsibility of this department to ensure that all employees
have the training to deliver some type of certified CPR or other
life saving in an emergency. Well this belief is partially correct.
Clearly, every employee, whether those with direct customer
contact or those who do not have customer contact, should be
able to deliver life-saving assistance to someone in need. But the
responsibility for ensuring this does not belong to the health and
safety department; it belongs squarely on the shoulders of senior
management.

Senior management are the ones who have a 'stewardship'
responsibility to the company, its employees and the customers
the organization comes in contact with and they are the ones who
control the budgets that impact the ability to train employees in
life saving. But when management decides not to make the decision to train people, the message is that a small investment in
training people to be certifiable in life saving is not as important
as being able to fend off the bad public relations and potential
legal actions that may then ensue. As I said before, this is a ludicrous position for management to put itself in – ask any shareholder whose shares will be devalued because of choosing
fire-fighting over prevention.

Management teams from all sectors, and from all business sizes,
need to figure out if they would rather prevent problems from
occurring, or have to deal with them . . . over and over again.
Next, they need to understand that investing in prevention is the

same as investing in the organization's future. And finally, they need to understand that if their company decides to opt out for continual fire-fighting behaviours, then they will be caught in a downward spiral that will, over time, potentially ruin their ability to be sustainable. And that is when the real fire-fighting starts.

When I was young, my father told me that an ounce of prevention is worth a pound of cure. And in business terms today, the same story is, '*a few euros of prevention training is worth potentially millions in bad PR and fighting law suits*'. The first lesson in risk prevention is learning to ask the right question, and it should be '*how can we prevent problems from occurring, instead of how to deal with them?*'

Questions

- In your organization, are problem efforts based on trying to solve it and then getting back to work, or on ensuring the solution never allows the problem to return?
- Do your managers enjoy fire-fighting problems? Are they addicted to it? Are they rewarded for it?

It's a matter of perspective

How to know what your options are

There are many organizations today that are at the fabled '*fork in the road*'. One direction leads to the land of high performance and organizational excellence, and the other direction leads to the valley of eternal crisis. Whilst most managers queried would come up with similar answers when asked the question, '*what do we need to do to achieve our company's vision?*', it is clear that there are many different views about how to do it. This is the organizational fork in the road, and sadly for many managers, there are no road signs to explain which direction leads to what.

For senior management, the choice can be a bit mystifying. Strategic plans that are deployed throughout organizations tend to have a singular message; a message that focuses on what needs to be done. But quite often, the methods used to achieve the strategic initiatives are left open to interpretation. This is one of the reasons why so few companies actually do realize the potential of their strategic plans. As with many problems that companies exist with, it is rarely the '*what we do*' that generates it; it is the '*how we do it*' that can muck things up.

The problem of differing perspectives on '*how to do* what needs to be done' results in fractionalized efforts, wasted time and resources, and can result in a demoralized workforce. And as most managers know who have been around on this planet for at least a week, these results are not good for business.

One of the management techniques to deal with this problem is to press harder for results, which can actually work, but it is a solution that is not sustainable, and using it causes more problems over time. The only real solution is to ensure that managers and employees have a clear picture of what needs to be done, how it should be done, and the rationale behind why. The reason is that in order to ensure that a strategy can actually be achieved, it is crucial to remove as much ambiguity from the decision-making process as possible.

In order to remove this ambiguity, senior management needs to do several things.

1   Be sure that the organizational strategy, if implemented effectively, will lead directly towards the desired future vision for the company. A strategy that does not mark out the path towards the desired future and at the same time, identify the ways to go down that path is just a waste of good paper.

2   Ensure that strategy identifies the few, vital activities that provide the greatest leverage in making forward progress. A strategic plan that identifies *all* the things (organizational-wide activities) that will need to be accomplished will do nothing but increase confusion and promote multiple perspectives on what is really most important to focus on. Use a prioritization tool to sort through the myriad of *possible important activities* to get the list down to the *three or four important activities* that will provide the greatest leverage.

3   Ensure that a clear process is identified that mid-managers and employees can follow that will allow them to identify and develop the next tier of activities. The process should follow a pattern of sub-activities, and when done effectively, will contribute to the successful completion of the vital few activities. A clear process to follow begins to eliminate ambiguity around how to decide what employees should focus their efforts on so that what needs to be accomplished *can* be accomplished.

4   Test to make sure that the picture that you want your people to see is the picture they see. This is not to say that the picture must be perfectly identical – having diversity in perspectives is

important in order to make sure that something stupid doesn't occur, but there is a big difference between perfect alignment, and alignment that ensures that the company gets to where it needs to go. Alignment in organizational initiatives and goals means alignment within parameters. It is akin to driving down the M4 (assuming you are there on a day when traffic actually moves). You may be headed out of London towards Heathrow Airport, but it doesn't mean that everyone has to be in the same lane, going the exact same speed, driving the exact same car, listening to the exact same music on the radio. Everyone on the motorway that day is headed in the same direction, but with some variation on the actual means to get there.

Having multiple perspectives in organizations is good. But it is only good if the perspectives are on the same goal, for the same reasons; and removing much of the ambiguity around what needs to be done, and for what reasons, can only help you get to where you want to go.

Questions

- If implemented effectively, will your organizational strategy take you to your organizational vision?
- Does your strategy have more than three or four organizational goals? Why?
- Does the organization have a clear process on how managers can best deploy the plan and next level responsibilities to their direct reports?
- Do you know if everyone in the organization 'sees' the same strategic picture? How do you know?

Putting ticks in boxes?

What can happen when change is not taken seriously

A senior manager asked me what I thought about IIP (Investing in People). Well, to tell the truth, I think what they are doing is pretty great, but it seems that many of the companies who subscribe to using IIP or any other well-meant initiative as a way to help them 'get better', are missing the point.

Whilst I agree that if organizations are to become better at creating environments in which their people can excel, one of my concerns is, 'why is it that their managers and employees were not able to excel in the first place?' What explicit and implicit policies and procedures did these organizations have in place that prevented their people from being able to *do the right thing, for the right reasons*? Yes, I am sure that there are managers out there who didn't know any better, and just assumed that to *manage*, they needed to do it by simply railing on their people to perform. That is like yelling at your children to not smoke or drink, and then going to the pub and having a pack of cigarettes with your lager. Managers don't demonstrate high performance because they are told to; they do it because *they see* the need to do it, and consequently, make the conscious choice to do so. They are connected to the business goals and they see how their contributions can help achieve them.

I also know that there are some managers out there who just don't have the requisite skills to manage and/or lead well. But that begs the question, 'who hired these people if they don't have the right skills?' Something is wrong here, and it is quite apparent that whilst we all want to have someone tell us we can put a 'tick' in the *we care about our people* box, simply putting ticks in boxes is not the answer.

Example 1: I know of a company that was so concerned that its people were doing the 'right thing' that it put in place a series of metrics to measure their effectiveness. So far, so good. But one of the objectives – making successful sales calls – manifested itself in the metric 'number of potential customers seen in one day' and the salespeople focused their efforts on going from one customer's office to another, and not on closing deals. Instead of the employees becoming more effective, they focused on getting the boxes ticked. Good intent; poor thinking.

Example 2: A company wanted to improve the speed with which it was able to introduce new products. Competition was beating it to the marketplace, and consequently the company was losing market share. Senior management sent out the message to reduce the delays in getting products into customers' hands, with the explanation that they couldn't afford delays. A relatively easy task, especially since the time spent testing the products was cut in one-half to accomplish the time reduction. The result was new products were introduced in less time than those of the competition . . . but soon rejected by customers for poor quality. Good intent; reckless implementation.

Example 3: A company I know of is trying really hard to help its employees take control of its destiny, so they instituted a programme with some title like 'creating our own future'. A good idea; get the people involved in the future of the company. But instead of the employees becoming motivated to contribute, they took the effort as just lip service on the part of senior management who, in the past, paid little attention to much other than getting the job done so they could report great earnings and look to the City. Yes, the programme was a big 'tick the box' effort, but that is all it was in the minds of the people who it was intended to engage. Good intent; bad planning.

Example 4: A company that brought in one of those IIP-type programmes to change the way the company was run. Assessors were running around like crazy, helping managers examine how they managed. They even told the managers how they could manage better. And when the programme was over, the company was able to say it had done it – it had invested in its people and life was now good. But the managers who were affected by the programme simply went back to business as usual; after all, the assessors were gone and they had targets to hit. Good intent, but missed the point.

All these examples are representative of organizational senior management who are missing the point of trying to get better. Instituting a programme targeted at improving company outcomes is only as good as management's ability to motivate its people. And when the employees simply see the programme as an exercise of *box-ticking*, the desired result is doomed. The only way that companies can get better at managing is to hold their managers accountable for not only the numbers, but their behaviours. Delivering high performance is a combination of both *what decisions are made*, and *how they are made*.

If a company is going to go through all the effort implied in investing in its people (something that *every company* needs to do), then it should make the effort worthwhile.

Defaulting on the choice to improve the decision-making process by going through the motions, and being able to 'tick the box' because now it can be seen to be investing in its people, is about as lame as senior management saying that poor performance is not its fault.

Questions

- Does your company invest in its people? Why?
- What is the expectation of those investments?
- When do you expect to see tangible results from the investment?

- What will you do if you do not see tangible results from your investment when you expect them?

Deciding who you are

Getting a grip on the power of changing behaviours

As I recall, SME is an abbreviation for Small and Medium Enterprise, but when you look at many of them, it appears that big business has a different view on the acronym. In many cases, big business treats SMEs as if the acronym stood for Subservient, Malingering and Error-prone. An example perhaps of arrogance and short-term memory on the part of the big guys?

Take a look at any big company. Now, look back through time and track down when the company actually began. Not too many were born the size of the National Health Service. Almost every company I know of began as an SME. The all-powerful Microsoft began as a couple of guys in some garage in America; Vodafone as we know it today was once a little spin-off from Racal; Hewlett-Packard started in a little wood shack; Google was begun by a couple of young kids who thought they had a better idea; even Volkswagen at one point was just a little car maker in Germany (as opposed to being a giant small car maker globally).

The whole issue of SMEs is one of scale. A company of 20 people is viewed as an SME compared to a company of 500; and a company of 500 might be viewed as an SME compared to one of 5,000; and a . . . well, you get the picture. But at some point in time, most companies were literally small and medium enterprises. Companies usually start because someone has what they think is a good idea. They take that good idea, and with commitment to it, go out and find customers who want or need it, and then they are in business. Starting a business is hard work, and when (and if) it makes it through the first year or two, it begins to run up against bigger businesses. And this is where having an SME becomes less than fun in some cases.

SMEs provide products and services that the big guys don't provide for one reason or another. Perhaps it is because the marketplace is too small, or perceived to be too small. (Remember the wisdom that came out of the mouth of the CEO of IBM in the 1960s – that the worldwide computer market was less than one dozen units?) SMEs deliver what no one else seems to want to deliver, and in many cases, they do it very well. Then why is it that many large companies treat SMEs like indentured servants that can be pushed around with (sometimes) unreasonable demands? The only reasons I can think of are (1) a sense of power, and/or (2) a short-term memory of the fact that without SMEs out there, many big companies would not be able to deliver what they promise to customers.

Having the 'power' over smaller companies can be a nice thing to have. You get to decide what you want, when you want it, how you want it, and what you will pay for it. All fine. But, by pressing SMEs too far, you run the risk of driving them into the ground, and without them, you might find yourself in a fine mess. Do you think you can just go off and find another SME to push around? Maybe. But word of mouth is a powerful thing, and if your company has a reputation of beating SMEs into submission, that word will get around, and what used to be a fertile ground of companies to pick and choose from may become a deserted wasteland.

If you (as a bigger business) are serious about ensuring that you can have good relationships with SMEs, there are a couple of things that you may want to consider. First, every once in a while, put yourself in their shoes. Think about what you are asking them to go through. Think about how you might react if the situation were reversed. Second, think about what would be an ideal SME supplier relationship – ideal meaning, if it worked perfectly, what would that relationship work like. Third, ring your SME suppliers and invite them in for a conversation. Ask them how they see the current relationship going, and ask them how you could make it better. The key here is that if the relationship is too one-sided (on either part), it won't work over time. Tell them what you are up against in your business, and see how they could help you. Yes, some of the obvious things that might come up will be costs, but they need to make money too. If they don't make a reasonable profit, they won't be able to invest in their ability to help you with quality, consistency, and the reduction of variation of the goods and services they provide to you.

Smaller companies, in most cases, are more flexible than larger ones. And flexibility usually means the ability to be responsive. Talk about how your needs (which may be perceived by SMEs as unreasonable demands) require your suppliers to respond quickly. See what you can do to help them be responsive.

The real trick of these types of conversations (for both sides) is to be open and honest about the relationship, how it is going, and where it is going. Talk as if you were talking to one of your business partners, because the reality is, that is exactly what your SME suppliers are; your partners in business. When they suffer, you will end up suffering too.

Questions

- Do you and your employees have a clear sense of what your company is all about?
- Do they understand the organizational purpose (mission)?
- Do they understand where the organization is going (its vision)?
- Do your suppliers and customers have the same understanding?
- What could you do to ensure they all know?
- What could you do to help them get a clearer picture?

The manager as coach

Why coaching is an integral part of enabling employees to change effectively

Of all the possible initiatives we can invoke for our employees, *Performance Improvement* is probably closest to the managerial Holy Grail. After all, it should bring measurable gains to the bottom line without the expense (or angst!) of changing personnel. One process stands at the heart of all performance improvement regimes I've seen – coaching.

Actually, I withdraw the word 'process' as too mechanistic a term for the things we could do to help people raise their game. Coaching is *not* training – we are not trying to impart previously unknown skills. Neither is coaching mentoring – we are not concerned with the individual's wider view of the company/the industry/their own career prospects, at least not here.

One of the most impactful ways for managers to help improve the performance of employees is through coaching. And yet, whilst this has been known and understood for some time, too often, one of three environments is seen in business today:

- coaching does not take place;
- coaching takes place, but it is done by people who don't have the skills to do so effectively;
- coaching takes place, but is curtailed to deal with cost constraints, either real or perceived.

Coaching could be one of the most misunderstood terms in business today. Coaching can best be considered as encouraging someone to do something different in order that they may do something else better. Now the good news from the manager's perspective is that they can and should function as coaches for their staff. The great news is that they themselves don't necessarily need to be world-class performers in the area under consideration. This is because the 'secret' of great coaching is not what you know as a coach, it's how you allow the individual to access what they know about themselves and harness it in the required direction.

This itself, I imagine, may come as a shock to many managers faced with coaching their employees. The fact is we can consider there to be two schools of coaching – and one of them is dangerous to all concerned!

Belief-based coaching is the common and traditional form of coaching. Its guides for practices are usually a mix of personal experiences, selected incomplete knowledge of current practices and self-belief in the only way to coach is 'my way – the way I was coached'. The accumulated knowledge of belief-based coaching is subjective, biased, unstructured, and mostly lacking in accountability. Belief-based coaching also includes half digested 'latest thinking' (but only when it agrees with what's already believed) and invariably this knowledge is incomplete and results in false and/or erroneous postulations. Belief-based coaching is unfortunately the foundation of most internal management development schemes. In this version of the world, organizations are closed systems resisting intrusions of contrary evidence that might alter the constancy of the beliefs and social structure. As ever with closed systems (if your memory of school physics stretches that far), disorder will only increase over time. Like the kids' game of *Chinese Whispers* well-meant messages will inevitably be corrupted and diverge from the organization's needs.

Evidence-based coaching is a relatively rare form of coaching. Its guides for practices are principles derived from reputable studies reported by authoritative sources. Evidence-based coaches have fewer such guides but what are included are highly predictive for accomplishing particular effects. Organizations here are open systems structured to constantly accept new knowledge and concepts. An example can be seen from the model formulated by Timothy Gallwey (*The Inner Game of Tennis*, New York, Random House, 1972).

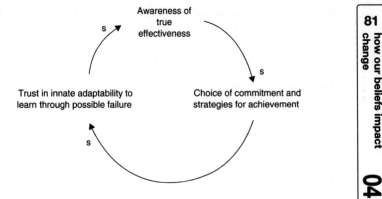

Figure 13

As illustrated in Figure13, he proposes that success arises from three resourceful states: *awareness* (knowing the present situation with clarity), *choice* (moving in a desired direction in the future) *and trust* (of one's inner resources as the essential link).

Putting this into the real world gives us some clarity on the issue. If, say, you wanted to play golf and had never played before then you would certainly need training to gather the basic information on techniques, fitness, etc. If, however, you could already play at some standard or other and your motivation was to improve your game then you would certainly employ the services of a coach. His or her job (having ascertained your knowledge of techniques, fitness, etc.) would then be to raise your awareness of what you were actually doing from the observer's standpoint. Not in a critical way – not good, not bad, just what you are doing.

The next step is to encourage the individual to choose what the required improvement is and commit to achieving it. This is a vital step. A manager (or anyone else) can't want you to be better anything like enough to overcome a lack of desire. The coach's input here then is facilitating the individual to rationalize and quantify the personal benefits resultant from the improved performance. Not, repeat not, the benefits as seen by the coach but those of the individual expressed in their own words. The coach's skill here is to prod and prompt and then to listen in silence again without inferring judgement of any kind.

The element of trust becomes central following the recognition of desire. It doesn't matter how the individual performed the task in the past, it doesn't matter how the coach would perform it, it doesn't matter how the most successful person in history performs it. The only thing that does matter is: what change has the individual identified as worth trying? It is the act of unself-consciously trying something different that is the key to unlocking performance improvement. It doesn't even matter if the change is successful. What the coach is looking for is the blessed state we inhabit as children when the burning desire to do something new is not hindered by the fear of failure. Failure doesn't matter except that it has the positive quality of not being the same (comparative) failure as before. The true learning state is where we try different approaches and accept or reject them *as leading to our desired improvement*. This is where the individual needs to trust that they have within themselves the wherewithal to progress through the journey of learning what works for them.

In essence, what we are doing here is unwinding the familiar competence/consciousness spiral and handing the opportunity to observe, and learn from it, to the individual *and the coach*. Success demands breaking the accepted paradigm that coaching is something I do to an individual and learning is something that just happens. Coaching is the conduit *not* the content.

Questions

- Does your company support coaching for employees?
- Are you, or have you been, a coach?
- Do you think your coaching has been effective?
- How do you know?
- What can you do to become a more effective coach?

The onset of panjandrums

What happens when we fall victim to our own self-importance

Of all the population groups that have been instrumental in creating environments in businesses today, I find one especially interesting. The group of people are the *Panjandrums*, and the environment that they have created is rather dire.

A panjandrum is, as defined by an online dictionary, '*an important personage or pretentious official*'. And from interviews that

I have conducted with quite a few organizations, it is clear that businesses are rife with them.

It is easy to spot them – panjandrums in organizations are the ones that have, as an apparent key competency, the ability to look incredibly busy, but accomplish little; they rush about exuding their importance, but have little to contribute that can make a difference; and would rather criticize someone for taking a risk than help them make better decisions. And whilst they may enjoy the glory of their position, their demonstrated behaviours of self-importance really do not provide value to their companies. And yet for some diabolical reason, they have managed to survive.

Let us think about what is really important in business. Yes, the obvious thing is to deliver sustainable performance; but underlying performance is the fundamental way in which organizations are managed and led. Clearly it is possible to 'hit the numbers' through a variety of ways, but the only way to sustainably achieve success is to demonstrate leadership behaviours.

Leadership behaviours are often mis-associated with just being the nice guy, or with all the soft, cuddly duck and bunny hugfests that loom large in the legend of leadership. But the reality is that real leaders can be tough, and quite often they are. The real way to distinguish the difference between leaders and managers is to look at how they inspire others; how they deal with problems; and how they view the world their respective companies exist in. Leaders look at challenges and accept them as opportunities. They are able to paint a compelling picture for others about why meeting the challenge is important. They ensure that employees have the skills and motivation to achieve greatness. And they see the world of business in a systemic way, with the real power of an organization coming through its relationships with suppliers, customers and employees. They avoid falling into the trap of reactive thinking when problems do arise, and instead focus on fundamental solutions that will eliminate the problem from occurring again.

And whilst all this may seem so terribly obvious, it is important to remember that at times, being a leader can be very hard work.

Our system of business today has resulted in massive pressures for short-term results and this, in turn, has driven short-term thinking. We have seen senior business people's decision-making being driven by external concerns and pressures. We have seen decisions that have literally put some companies out of business. And we have seen organizational cultures devastated by panjandrum-like behaviours. And yet, there are organizations out there that do stay focused on their missions; that are able to move successfully towards the achievement of their visions; and where environments are created in which the employees and the company can realize its potential.

The challenge belongs to each of us to make the choice. Do we want to work for, and lead, an organization where we can feel and know that our actions contribute in a positive way, or do we want to be a panjandrum, just slogging through the day in our self-importance, avoiding taking a risk for fear of being held accountable? To make this choice even clearer, do you want to be appreciated and recognized for being a leader, or will you be content to be the local panjandrum? Before you make the choice, think about what type of person others think you currently are, and what type of person you would like to report to in your organization. It should make your choice a bit easier.

Cutting programmes designed to ensure long-term company stability and success is nothing more than short-term, reactive thinking. When some research has shown that the single most powerful differentiator for corporate success is the speed with which a company's employees can learn, this type of cost-cutting represents thinking that is myopic at best, and more appropriately, corporate lunacy.

Most certainly, when times are tough, costs must be monitored very closely, and excessive costs must be cut away. But just because training is one of the most obviously visible costs that are available to go after, it doesn't mean that management needs to take the easy way out. In most cases, this is a result of a lack of real leadership in organizations. Leaders are different from managers; management is all about keeping things within control, but leadership is all about creating environments in which organizations can realize their potential.

If your organization is suffering from unacceptable profit levels, think twice before you fall into the management trap of whacking away at easily visible costs, especially when cutting them may result in serious unintended negative consequences that few organizations can recover from. Or, if you think that short-term, myopic reactive thinking is the way to go, then just don't be surprised when the long-term future of your company simply disappears over time.

Questions

- Are there managers in your company who believe that because they have managerial responsibilities (and titles) they are able to think differently about organizational challenges?
- Are senior and mid-managers open to feedback on their performance?
- Are they open to feedback on their communications and leadership skills?
- What might happen if they are not open to feedback?

Good news, bad news

Making sure we really understand

Imagine this scenario. The good news is that you have recently begun your new job as the head of the company. You survived the hiring process and the interviews with the Board, and actually were gratified to know that the Board Chair was supportive of everything you spoke about doing. The bad news is that already you are running into problems with the Board. So much for having a honeymoon period in the job where you could begin to make your mark.

This scenario has happened more times that it should, and I recently spoke with a friend who was in this exact situation. He had been brought in as CEO for a small service organization that was, to put it bluntly, stuck. The previous CEO (who is also the Board Chair and company owner) had done a fantastic job getting his company off the ground, and had even made substantial headway in helping the organization realize its potential. But as so often happens, the growth performance began to stall, and to his credit, he decided that the company needed some new leadership.

Differing views that a Board has quite often stem not because the Board wasn't aware of what you were going to do, but more often when the words don't match with the reality. In the case of my friend (and in most situations where the Board is headed up by the ex-CEO), everything he wanted to do was discussed prior to his hiring. And in addition, the Board actually hinted that specific structural shifts should be made, all of which the new CEO supported. But when he actually started making these changes and acting as the CEO, the Board members began to voice their concerns.

This is not that different than a father who is quite open about the fact that what he wants most is for his children to make their own decisions about their lives, but when they start making them, the father starts mumbling with comments like, 'well, this isn't the way I would have done it', or 'when I was your age . . .'.

Once a Board is comfortable with its hiring choice for the CEO position, it needs to let go and put trust in its new person and in its own decision. But to be fair, the new CEO needs to be extremely thoughtful about his or her upward communications.

Being plopped in the CEO's chair, regardless of what verbal support you have been given during the hiring process, is not a licence to go off and do what you thought they wanted you to do without some effective communication. Boards, especially just after a new CEO has been brought in, need relatively constant reassurance that their choice was right. This holds especially true when the Board Chair is the owner and previous CEO. The new guy needs to recognize that if he doesn't deliver some successes quickly, the Board Chair may begin to second guess itself and decide to remove the new CEO and find someone else. If he or she does deliver some successes quickly, the Board Chair may begin to feel that too much success too quickly will show everyone that he or she should have gotten out of the senior position sooner. It is almost a no-win situation. But there are things that can be done to avoid a potentially looming crisis.

1   A new CEO should provide frequent status reports for the Board on what he or she is doing, why he or she is doing it, and what progress had been made. This seems like a given, but in many cases, the frequency of the updates falls off as the new CEO senses that it is more important to crank on the business than it is to keep the Board abreast of progress.

2   A new CEO should provide his or her updates in a structured format. A format that works well is something developed by Barbara Minto in London. Ms Minto developed a process known as 'structured thinking', and the process is perfect for using for CEO to Board updates. For each update, the CEO should begin with the situation the company is in; followed by the things that complicate that situation. This is then followed by a question such as 'based on where we are, what is the most appropriate action we can take?' And then you provide the answer, followed by either inductive or deductive reasoning for why your solution makes sense. This process works well because

the situation/complication area demonstrates that you know what you are talking about, and as the Board Chair (ex-CEO) probably recognizes what you have described, his comfort level will increase in the knowledge that you are not in some deluded state. When you then provide your solution to the situation, followed by either inductive or deductive reasoning, the listener should be able to understand why your solution is the most appropriate one.

3   Ask the listener (it is the Board Chair who used to be the CEO remember) if he or she has any concerns or questions about the direction you are taking. After you have given him or her the opportunity to talk, say, 'this is what I am hearing you say', followed by what the Chair has said. This will demonstrate that you are listening empathically and again reassure the Chair that the choice to bring you in was appropriate. When you respond, put your response once again in a format of 'answer followed by reasoning for that answer'.

4   Share your priorities with the ex-CEO. Make sure that you can explain a rationale for prioritizing activities in the way that you have so that there is a reduced risk of him or her becoming disillusioned by your decisions.

5   At the end of each meeting, re-confirm the next scheduled update and propose specific topics to discuss.

The whole reason to follow a structure for Board Chair (or whole Board) updates is to demonstrate that you are the right person to do the job, and to help them become comfortable with their choice. You still may be in an environment in which an ex-CEO believes that he or she could have done things better, but the reality is that if they could have, they would still be in that position.

Questions

- If you have recently accepted a new position, are you and those that hired you in alignment on the achievement of the goals you discussed when you were interviewed?
- If not, why do you think that there is a gap in alignment?
- What are you doing to help close that gap?
- How often do you provide updates for your supervisors?
- Do the updates help to close the gap in alignment or exacerbate it?

Too busy to see the oncoming train?

What happens when we are blinded by our own unwillingness to see

The Institute of Directors recently released the results of a study they commissioned to see how much effort businesses were putting into getting ready for the future. The meaning is clear: getting ready for the future is all about dealing with change and avoiding potential crises. When I read some of the study results, I was floored. Sixty-nine per cent of the respondents to the question, *'what factors inhibit future thinking in your organization?'* stated that they were *'too busy'*. Too busy to figure out what the future might bring? Wake up lads; the light at the end of the tunnel just may be an oncoming train named 'The Crisis Express'.

According to the report, 30 per cent of the respondents mentioned that they had 'a lack of in-house expertise', and another 31 per cent cited 'inadequate resources' as the reason that their ability to see into the future was inhibited. These responses raise a very serious question – *how can organizations expect to survive into the future when no one is trying to determine what that future might bring?*

Yes, managers today are probably busier than ever, but busy doing what? Most of the managers I speak with seem to have their diaries filled with ongoing, recurring problems that have never been really solved. They are inundated with assignments and responsibilities that feed the addiction to reactive thinking and fire-fighting. Just look at the stories in the media: budget airlines that don't seem to care if they alienate customers because they assume that other customers will fill the seats; energy company managers that are so busy patting themselves on the back for high profits that they forget that it wasn't their decision-making excellence that generated them, but instead the global demand for oil; and senior managers who are quick to say their heads are on the line, but then shun the responsibility for organizational performance. It might be time for them to either change the way they do business and set priorities, or for customers and shareholders to make their voices heard more loudly.

The ability, or in many cases willingness, to look to the future can be a make-or-break competency for companies. Behaviours and skills that were acceptable a dozen years ago just don't cut it in any more. Being 'too busy' to try to put clarity on potential scenarios that a business may face is akin to driving your car at high speed day and night, just to clock up as many miles as possible. Sure, you may see your odometer climb quickly, but if you don't stop once in a while to check the engine or put petrol in, you will end up on the side of the road sitting watching your competitor cruise past. To put it plainly, there simply is no excuse for not trying to understand what the future might bring, unless of course, you don't care. And in some companies I know, that is the case.

The average tenure in a senior organizational position today is declining. CEOs seem to last as long as summer in England, and when the new one arrives, the first piece of business appears to be how to make his mark on the company. That behaviour is almost understandable; they are given high-paying jobs with lots of responsibility and are under pressure to deliver the performance results the last incumbent wasn't apparently able to deliver. But seldom do we see new leaders begin by focusing on ensuring that the business will survive long after they have retired. Instead, the focus is on driving short-term results that distract from the larger issue of sustainability.

Over 30 years ago, the people at Royal Dutch Shell did planning based not only on what they needed to accomplish, but also on *what might happen in the future*. They were the only energy company who had plans ready to deal with what we know as OPEC. And these plans enabled them to be prepared when the price of crude oil skyrocketed. They were thinking in terms far longer than the literal tomorrow. Unfortunately, this ability within Shell has disappeared, as now they, as we have seen, seem to have had a focus on managing the market expectations through number manipulation. The story of GEC-Marconi is another prime example. When Lord Weinstock was the head of GEC, the company kept thinking about what the future might bring. No, it wasn't sexy and cool to do that, but the company was profitable and stable and positioned for the future. And then Weinstock was sent away and new people came in who were blinded by the immediate future. And as shareholders of Marconi can attest to, the once proud company is just a shadow of its previous self, and probably lucky to be in business at all.

Does Ryanair really think that they will always have enough customers with their apparent policy of 'do it our way or go find another carrier?' Are the decision-makers at BP that sure that the price of oil will never again go down? Do the senior people at BA think that just because they used to be the best, they will always be in business? What are these companies going to do if they are wrong? Come on lads, let's use some common sense and realize that the future is not guaranteed.

Senior management need to rethink some of their priorities. Planning for the future is just as important as planning for next quarter, and not having people looking long term is inexcusable in today's business world. Indeed, the light at the end of the tunnel just might be an incoming train.

Questions

- How does your organization decide on its priorities?
- How does it communicate these decisions to managers and employees?
- How does it ensure that these priority decisions are actually delivered upon?

05

dealing with influencing factors

In this chapter you will learn:

- how to influence others
- how to build and retain buy-in
- how to avoid letting external forces kill motivation

External factors can both help and aggravate the ability of an organization to survive ongoing changes and crises. The ability to balance both internal needs and external requests and assumptions about what is important can make or break an organizational capability to survive.

Communications: art or science?

How communications can impact change efforts

If we have learnt anything about communications, it is the fact that communications is both science and art. Science because we have tested and learnt communications techniques that have proved to be more effective than others; and we have used these learnings to increase the effectiveness of what we do. Art because regardless of what we know, sometimes everything we have learnt over time about how to ensure effective communications seems to fail for reasons that are beyond our control. Or so we would like to believe.

All this is a bit complicated by the fact that many senior managers in organizations from all sectors, believe that they are brilliant communicators. I have seen quite a few senior managers who are keen to see that communications are managed effectively . . . except when it comes to their own. I have worked with many senior managers who are convinced that communications professionals are a necessary evil, and whilst they may appear to listen to their advice, they, for the most part, believe that the professionals are there to help *everyone else*.

Recently, I sat in on a corporate communications event in which many hours had been put in to make sure that *the message* was spot on. Various scripts had been written and tested, with a final version being supplied to the speaker (a senior manager) two days beforehand so that he could feel comfortable with what he was to say. And on the day of the event, he delivered the talk. But an informal survey at the coffee machines afterwards showed that very few people actually *heard* the message that had been delivered.

When the senior manager became aware of the less-than-enthusiastic responses to his talk, his reaction was quite predictable; the communications content was poor; the slides that had been prepared for him were worthless; and the employees in the audience were 'slackers who weren't worth sharing information with'. He told his communications people to *'get their act together, and do it now'*. The expression 'there is more going on than meets the eye' pretty much summed up what had happened that day.

The organization had been undergoing some pretty severe changes, with ongoing reorganization being the only constant that the employees could be confident of; and because of this, the organizational climate had been falling faster than the stock market during an oil crisis. One of the outcomes of this fall was that the employees' trust of corporate communications was at an all time low. Whilst it was clear that effective communications were extremely critical at this point in the company's history, it was also clear that the dynamic complexities of the message and the way it was communicated needed to be addressed.

There is no doubt that when the senior manager gave his talk, everyone heard the same words, but it was also clear that what registered in their minds varied wildly from the words themselves. It was decided to find out exactly what was going on by utilizing Chris Argyris' 'left-hand column'. Thus it might be possible to find out what employees are really *hearing* when messages are being delivered.

When the manager's next talk was prepared, key points were noted and printed on the right-hand side of single sheets of A4 paper. The left-hand column was left blank. Employees who were scheduled to be in the audience during the talk were identified, and several of them who were known to have influence amongst their peers were each given a copy of the form as they walked into the conference room. Their instructions were simple: when the manager spoke the words that were printed on the form (the words on the right-hand column of the paper), each of them should write down in the left-hand column what he or she was really *hearing* (see Figure 14). The forms had been designed so that none of the people asked to fill them out could be identified later, in order to ensure an open and honest picture of how the talk was received. Afterwards, the papers were collected and looked at, with the results being more than alarming. It was clear that one of the reasons that the employees were not *hearing* what was being communicated was that there was a distinct lack of trust in much of what was being said. Employees would sit politely whilst listening to the messages, bobbing their heads up and down at the appropriate times, but as they were pre-focused on what they called 'management babble' the actual messages were lost. Effectively managing employee communications in

What was 'heard'	What was said
What does he mean 'unforeseen'? Isn't part of your job to know what is going on and stay ahead of the competition? I'll bet you still get your bonus. Talk about a double-standard!	'Due to an unforeseen increase in competition, we will not be able to hit our quarterly targets. And because of this, we may not be able to pay out the bonuses we had planned on.'
Is he going to tighten up and improve his own decision-making?	'We are all going to have to tighten things up and improve our performance . . .'
All in it together? You sit in your posh offices and don't have a clue what it is like to do the real work in the company.	'We are all in this together.'
They have been pushing back getting us up-to-date equipment for three years. How are we expected to compete when they cut training and stop investments to help us hit the targets?	'Because of our financial shortfall, our investments in equipment and technology may have to be postponed until next year . . .'
What makes them think the economy is going to get better soon? They didn't even know how good the competition is.	'. . . when the economy is better and we are back on track.'
None of these guys are even fit to lead us out of this mess. It was them who got us into the mess; how can they get us out?	'I and the entire leadership team are behind you 100%.'

Figure 14

this type of environment can become a challenge on a par with walking on water. And unfortunately, it happens too often.

When shown the information gleaned from the left-hand column forms, the senior manager once again went into defensive mode and after recriminations against his employees, communications staff, and the world as a whole, offered his own suggestion;

reduce the level of communications. *'These people aren't worth communicating with'*, was his rationale. This, of course, would have been the worst solution possible.

The best solution can be found by looking at what the employees *heard* during the talk, and what was causing that. Each of us internalize communications through our own mental model filter. The employees in this case were filtering whatever was communicated through a filter laden with beliefs that senior management wasn't doing their job, and weren't even competent to do those jobs. The manager was filtering the feedback through a filter that was laden with beliefs that the employees shouldn't have to know everything that was going on in the organization, and, because they didn't *hear* his actual messages, were probably incompetent as well. The real challenge facing the communications people was to get the two sides to really listen to each other.

Because of the existing disconnection between what was being communicated and what was being heard, the news about what was going on in the front-lines wasn't filtering its way up in the organization. For example, there was a story that surfaced on the BBC about the largest nuclear warship in the Russian navy, the *Peter the Great*. Naval inspectors had been on the ship, and after several days, ordered the ship back to Murmansk for urgent repairs due to the fact that *'where the admirals onboard worked, then everything on the ship was fine, but where they didn't go, the condition of the ship was so dire that there was great risk to the crew and the ship itself'*. The crew of the ship had known that providing 'bad news' was not a good thing and, consequently, hadn't reported all the problems the ship was having to the admirals. What occurred on the *Peter the Great* was not all that dissimilar to the previous story about the corporate communications dilemma.

Employees and managers alike need to have a communications environment in which there is a common understanding of what is good and bad news. Good news – *what we believe we want to hear* – is fine. But what we consider bad news – *what we don't like to hear* – is in reality good news as well. For the only really bad news is *not knowing*. Creating an environment in which employees and managers are *able* to communicate effectively with each other can be the greatest challenge for communications professionals.

Questions

- How much effort is expended in your organization to understand what others are saying in meetings and presentations?

- How can you ensure that the words of a message are heard, as well as the meanings behind those words?
- What happens when people mis-understand key messages?
- What happens to the people who do not understand?

Trying to stay dry

Why everyone in the organization must actively participate in changing

During the 2005 elections in Germany, Norbert Walter, the chief economist for Deutsche Bank, was quoted as saying 'There's the old German saying, "*Wash my fur, but don't get me wet*".' He may have been talking about the fear of change on the part of Germans, but the statement applies to employees of most businesses today . . . all over the world.

We all know that change is the only constant in business, or by now we should know this. I can't think of the last time I heard that change is not something that employees will be subject to. But at the same time, whilst we may accept that change is here to stay in our organizations, we sure don't like it when we are the ones who are asked to do the changing.

Being in an organization that is moving in a direction you don't like is like being on a plane that is flying from London to Reykjavik – if, when you realize what the destination is, you decide you don't want to go there, your choices are to either (A) get off the plane (a hazardous thing to do at 12,000 metres); (B) close your eyes and hold your breath thinking that the pilot will somehow sense your feelings and reroute the plane to Palma (as if that would happen just for you); or to (C) get with the programme and understand why going to Reykjavik could be a valuable experience.

There are several problems with the way that organizations introduce change to their people.

1   *If no real case for change is given, there will be little chance that the employees will buy into the effort.* A case in point can be found in the global energy companies around the world today. Most cases for change involve lack of necessary profits, but in the case of the oil companies, there seems to be no end to the current gusher of profits that the companies are experiencing due to the price of crude oil. All the talk we used to hear about incompetence in decision-making has disappeared and instead, managers

are just reeling in the glory of how smart they must be to be generating all this money (which of course, is not the reason they are flush with money. They are profitable because of external forces that have driven the price of oil to unheard of limits, resulting in massive profits for them). This is what we call, being at the right place at the right time; and one can only wonder if they will take this opportunity to make the changes that should be made so as to not waste the profits. Examine your case for change, and if it is difficult to find, look at some of the systemic ramifications of continuing to do business as it is being done today.

2   Too often, *employees do not see the benefits from the change effort* – benefits that they should experience directly and indirectly. If employees cannot see 'what is in it for them', the chances that they will ever buy-in will be almost non-existent. Employees are not stupid, and they, for the most part, will believe that change is taking place for the sake of change unless you can help them see the benefits that will come to them. And in most cases, this does not just mean more money. Employees are keen to know if the change effort will help them learn and grow, help create an environment in which they could become more motivated, and increase the chances that the company will become more sustainable (and consequently, they might be able to keep their jobs). Help employees see what is in it for them if they buy into, and become committed to, the change effort.

3   *In many cases, change is perceived to be just another corporate programme*, and not an underlying parameter that all organizations need to deal with. Programmes come and go, and if the employees believe that change is just another one of those, many of them will develop a bunker mentality and try to wait it out. The defence mechanisms that they use to keep change at bay are complex, but usually effective. This results in depressed employee morale, wasted time and resources, and falling performance. By having a consistent message that every day change will need to be occurring in the organization, employees will be able to shift their mental models to accept change for what it really is . . . a way to improve an organization's ability to survive, to grow and to prosper.

Dealing with organizational change is much like what Franklin Roosevelt said years ago: '*the only thing we have to fear is fear itself*'. It is the responsibility of senior management to make sure that organizational change and fear do not have to be used in the same context. This, however, will require a change in mindsets on the part of management as well as those of employees. Unfortunately, it is apparent that many senior managers in organizations today in the UK must have been raised to believe that Norbert Walter statement about Germans is right, and they don't want to get wet either.

Questions

- Do you (and your peers) have a good understanding of where your organization is going, why it is moving in this direction, and how it will get there?
- What is an unintended consequence of missing or mixed messages about the changes that are occurring?
- What can you do to help alleviate the missing or mixed messages?
- Are you comfortable with providing upward feedback in your organization about communications?
- If so, how can you share that 'lack of comfort' with your boss?

Events dear boy, events

How we can be deluded into thinking some crises are not our fault

When he was Prime Minister, Harold Macmillan was asked by a young journalist after a long dinner what can most easily steer a government off course, he answered '*Events dear boy, events.*' In short, politics can be unpredictable. And based on many of the results we see in the business pages, the same holds true for business. Unfortunately, however, in business, it is not the results that are unpredictable; it is the way in which management plan (or doesn't plan) for events, or the way in which they react to them.

Not that many years after America On-Line began to make headway in the US market, someone in its organization came up with the ultimate marketing plan: send out CD-ROMs with a free download programme for the AOL online service to virtually everyone in America. On the surface, this was a relatively brilliant plan – make installation and enrolment in AOL's online service painless so that the company would be able to see a dramatic increase in its customer base. But events took over and the plan turned into a near disaster. The events that took over were the millions of people who actually accepted the offer and after installing AOL onto their computers, they all went online. The mass influx of customer activity overtaxed the AOL system and suddenly they were risking alienating many of the existing and new customers, putting the overall plan at risk. Could this have been anticipated? Probably, but the point is that no one apparently did.

British Airways had been suffering from bad press due to unhappy customers that had suffered through delays and cancelled flights due to work stoppages. So the people at BA put together a plan to reverse the bad image and get more people in their seats again. But as with the experience that AOL had, events mucked up BA's plans. Gate Gourmet, one of the largest sub-contractors that BA uses, was under serious pressure from the airline to reduce costs, and part of the food supplier's solution was to cut back on its workforce. But when the news broke, the Gate Gourmet workforce at Heathrow Airport decided to respond with a work stoppage. And the work stoppage spread to the baggage handlers that BA uses, and the airline's arrivals and departures at the airport ground to a halt. BA's plan to recover from bad press was suddenly destroyed by the work stoppage, and subsequent queues of people whose flights were cancelled, and once again, BA was in the news for not meeting customers' needs.

Throughout 2005, Diageo, the drinks maker, had been on a roller coaster, but overall, the stock price had increased quite a bit in the past twelve months. Things were looking up, and then the virtual parade of hurricanes went marching through the south-eastern United States, chopping away at demand, and consequently, sales. And whilst some might say that hurricanes are not exactly predictable, the very fact that they can occur means that there should have been a contingency for short-term drops in sales. Another 'event' that has played havoc with Diageo, and quite a few other companies has been the dramatic increase in the price of oil.

Whilst these examples of events that have created problems for companies may seem to have been out of the realm of anticipating them, the real point is that most organizations are not the best at planning for contingencies, regardless of how obscure they seem at the time.

Planning for contingencies is not all that difficult, but the first step is to be aware of what *might* occur. To do this requires a shift in the traditional thinking processes. Encourage your people to not only come up with the intuitive events that might occur, but to also think counter-intuitively. Quite often, this can be done by making a list of the very worst things that could happen to your organization, and then work backwards to figure out what events might possibly cause them.

Next, identify what you can do to either *prevent* the events from happening, or to *mitigate* the negative effects that may accompany them. Follow this with a plan of what you will do if you find yourself in the middle of something you won't like.

Or, there is another option. Just spend some time standing in front of a mirror practising saying to your shareholders, '*Poor performance? Well, it is because of events dear shareholder, events*'. And then spend some time getting your CV up to date, because you just may need it.

Questions

- Is your organization driven by events, or do you have a plan that is being followed?
- What happens when unforeseen things occur that may cause you to divert from the plan?
- Why are some events not anticipated? What is the cost of not knowing what might occur?

What do they expect will occur?

Waking up to the reality of the situation the organization faces

We have seen this happen over and over again: senior business managers make strong commitments to learning and personal skill improvement, but when something runs amiss with projected profits, all the promises and commitments disappear faster than lemmings rushing to the cliff edge. These behaviours send several signals to managers and employees . . . and the signals can be devastating over time.

I have interviewed quite a few managers at companies that have seen this happen – CEOs pledge that learning and training is the most important thing a company can do to ensure a long-term future (which is true), but when profits fall, training is the first thing to be hacked away; and when training disappears, most learning opportunities disappear with it. Reactions seem to fall into several categories of statements.

- *The long-term future of the company is not really important apparently.*

This reaction – when employees are told that the only way to ensure long-term success is to learn faster than the competition, but training is cut as soon as things are tough – leads to the conclusion that management is only focused on the short term. Cancelling training programmes will undoubtedly save companies money, but it is just a demonstration of reactive thinking on the part of the senior decision-makers. When profits fall, or don't meet expectations, cuts probably do need to be made, but cutting training is like amputating your child's legs if he falls off his bicycle. Sure, he won't fall anymore, but he will also never be able to ride again.

- *The senior guys just don't get it, and are not worth us putting in all the extra effort they ask us to do.*

When training programmes are cut, some organizational senior managers just expect that employees will continue to learn on their own. Well, fair enough. If employees recognize the need for life-long learning, it stands to reason that they would continue to seek learning opportunities on their own. However, the problem is that self-directed learning can stray from what employees need to learn to be more effective in their jobs. Most organizations need to invest in training their people, especially new employees, in how the company does what it does. They need to train employees, especially long-time employees, in change and how best to deal with it. They need to train all employees, especially management, in how to communicate more effectively. If the company doesn't sponsor this training, the chances that the employees will learn it are slim.

- *Senior management cannot be trusted to keep their word.*

This might be the scariest of the signals that employees glean when training is stopped. If the senior managers can break a promise to train people – so that they can help ensure that the company will remain competitive and not be subject to profit shortfalls – what other promises will they break is a common question; a question that is asked just before employee commitment begins to plummet. Any organization that does not have employees that are committed to the company direction and the team that is leading the strategic initiatives that should achieve a company vision is doomed to ongoing fluctuations in ability.

Questions

- Does your company invest in training and skill enhancement for managers and employees?
- Is it enough?
- Do managers actually participate in the training, or do they just expect that it is for non-managers?
- What signal is sent to employees if managers do not participate in training?
- Is the training focused on typical 'hard skills' or does it also include 'soft skills' such as communications, organizational vision and values, interpersonal relationships, and thinking and influencing skills?

Oh, the money thing

How external influences can drive real and perceived crises

The banking industry in the UK seems to be becoming, to paraphrase the late Hunter S. Thompson, *'a cruel and deep money trench, where banks' policies are infallible, and customers are treated as if they had ebola. And then there is a darker side to it'*.

I met a CEO who told a frightful story. It seems that his company was between the proverbial rock-and-a-hard-place. His business has been growing quite well, but the more it has expanded, the more he has needed to go to banks for short-term financing (for cash flow) and long-term financing (for additional equipment). This in itself wasn't a problem. His problem was that the banks always seemed to want cash as collateral for loans. But that was why he was going to them. Why would a bank want cash to collateralize a loan when the lack of it was the problem? Even the man's bank manager told him that his company is doing well and that there were no underlying problems that would prevent them from making the loans. They just don't want to do so without cash as collateral. Am I missing something here? If his company had the cash, why would he even go to the bank? His problem was fast approaching crisis stage.

I am sure that his bank had some good reason (well, good in their mind) why they weren't keen on lending him more money, but the bottom line is that one of the things that banks do is to loan money, especially to small and medium businesses. That is how small and medium sized businesses grow to become big businesses. Yes, lending money to a business does have risks associated with it, but to ask for an equal amount of cash as collateral seems a bit daft. Are banks today so risk averse that they only want to deal with the big guys? Or is it that they simply want to keep up their run of exceptionally high profits, and lending to the little guys isn't as profitable? It should be. Even with all the current and planned banking legislation out there, with the assortment of semi-stealth service charges that are used, profitability for banks is as certain as BP being profitable with the price of oil over $75 a barrel.

The CEO has been working with several banks for the past few years, and each of them sends him monthly statements of the fees they are charging him for the *service they are providing*. Nice – *the service*. His company is charged a management fee, interest on existing loans, service charges for cheque processing, service charges for credit card purchases, service charges for monitoring his cash flow, and service charges for just about everything else. I have seen some of these charges, and it is no wonder that he needs to borrow more – the monthly outgoing is unbelievable. So what did I tell him? Easy, just go to a different bank. Well, not so easy. The banks must have some secret handshake thing going on because every bank he talks to tells him the same thing. *The same thing!* Maybe the banks have somehow managed to become a bit psychic and are able to read the minds of their competitors. If my new friend doesn't like what his current bank is willing to do, he should just be able to go to its competition, but *there is no competition* it appears.

To top it all off, the way that consumers are being treated by banks puts a whole new spin on the term 'customer service'. Recently, when I needed some cash, I stopped at a convenient cash machine and after typing in my security number, and requesting some money, was told by the machine that there would be an eight-pound charge for the service. Eight pounds? What planet are these guys from? Had there not been another cash machine a block away (one where there was no charge), I would have been stuck. Yes, banks need to make money for their shareholders, just like any other business, but there is something wrong with this picture. I was tempted when writing this to look up 'customer service' in an online dictionary, but was afraid it would say something like, 'the verbiage used by banks to describe how you can be mugged legally'.

Banks make money because they provide a service. Whether lending money to businesses so that they can grow, or providing services to you and me (like cash machine access) so our lives can be a bit better. But as a consumer of these services, I am certainly feeling like someone who the banks treat as an ongoing revenue source, and at the same time, feeling abused for the *privilege* of doing so.

I read the papers. I am keenly aware of the profit levels that banks are enjoying today. But I guess I assumed that because of not only their profitability, but also because of their charters, they would be a bit keener to help a local business grow to establish a stronger presence in the community – greater potential for long-term banking relationships. I assumed that they would want to help more people become employees of a growing business – greater potential for getting more depositors. I assumed that they would want to encourage both consumers and businesses to use more of their services, but by treating them in the way that they do, it is becoming frightfully clear that banks want to have their cake and eat it too.

If banks want to continue to make profits, whilst at the same time, retain their customers, conversations need to take place to figure out how businesses can borrow money to stay in business.

Go sit with your (hopefully friendly) banker and find out what its 'rules' for borrowing are. Then explain your situation, and ask him or her how together, the two of you can ensure that you are able to remain in business and continue to grow so he or she can count on you and your money staying in that bank. And if that doesn't work, then do what you would do with any other supplier of services – go shopping for another supplier.

Questions

- Does your organization suffer from an inability to ensure it can keep up with growth plans?
- What are the 'rules' for communicating internally and externally in your organization?
- Do your managers participate in training to help them listen and communicate more effectively?

part 3

stories from the workplace

06

getting the
work done
and surviving

In this chapter you will learn:

- how to survive ongoing change programmes
- how to ensure your team can be effective
- how to avoid self-fulfilling failure

The front-line of any organization is where the real work gets done, and in most cases, it is also where change and crisis really hit home. Being able to get the work of the company done whilst dealing with change and crisis is a critical issue for all organizations.

Getting their heads around what it is like

Understanding the challenge of changing behaviours

I have always found it pretty amazing that those in management quite often just assume that employees should be able to deal with all the changes that organizations go through. Yes, managers have to deal with change as well, but for some reason, many managers still assume that because they manage to survive the changes they go through, the rest of the employees shouldn't have a problem surviving as well. This could be a fair mental model, after all, being a manager quite often isn't that much fun. However, if you are a senior manager, and really want to get a sense of what everyone else in the organization is up against, the next time you have a senior management meeting, try this out.

Have the senior managers stand up and pair off. It doesn't matter who pairs up with whom, just get them to pick someone else in the group and stand with them. Next, have each pair face each other.

Now, have the pairs of people turn around so their backs are facing each other so they can't see each other. And then tell them to change something about their appearance. Actually, change three things about their appearance. They can undo their ties, they can mess up their hair, they can take their glasses off (assuming they wear glasses), they can pull their shirts out, they can do any three things that will change their own appearance. Now have them turn back so they face each other. Yes, and have them identify the three things their partners had changed.

After they have all had a bit of fun with this, tell them to once again turn away from each other and change three more things. No, they shouldn't just change things back to the way they were; change three more things about their appearance. Then have them turn around and identify their partner's changes again. (In most cases, the changes are identifiable, and the pairs of people do have a good time 'playing this game'.)

But now, have them do it all once again. Yes, turn away from each other and change three more things. By now, you will begin to find that they are not having quite as much fun, usually because they think they are running out of things that they can change. And if you have to do it a fourth time, do it. And what do you find?

The senior management team will be struggling to both deal with this exercise of constant change, and the ability to keep changing can begin to make the game not fun anymore. And this is just what your employees are up against. Employees feel that they are the brunt of most change initiatives. They feel that just when management gets through with one change initiative, another one comes along, quite often before the previous one has really reached completion.

Will light bulbs go on in the heads of senior management? Perhaps, but perhaps not. It really doesn't make a difference . . . what you have done is given them the opportunity to experience what everyone else in the organization experiences, and if they don't learn from that, well, that is another issue.

Questions

- Are the senior managers in your organization as open to change as they expect you to be?
- How do you know this?
- If they are not, what can be done to help them?
- What is the signal that is sent by a 'do as I say and not as I do' message?

Why things don't get done

Why many crises seemingly come out of nowhere

In preparation for this book, I took time to meet with quite a few managers from different organizations, from different sectors, and of companies of varying sizes, and they have all expressed the same concern: things just aren't getting done in their organizations . . . and they can't figure out why. The problem is complicated in each situation because they all report that they have sound strategic planning processes, and managers who are, for the most part, competent in their jobs.

Sitting in with these managers, it became clear where their problems lie. Yes, they all had strategies that made sense; each of them had ensured that resources would be made available for the implementation of the strategic goals; and yet, the level of assigned and agreed-to responsibilities for the implementation of the goals was vague, if not invisible. And to complicate things, in my meetings, when the manager would raise concerns about things not getting done, others would agree that this was a major problem. But I didn't hear at any of the meetings anyone standing up and saying he (or she) would be willing to accept responsibility for changing things.

You may have been in similar meetings: someone says that there is a problem; some people come up with possible solutions to the problem; almost everyone agrees that one solution is the best and that it should be used to solve the problem . . . and then they move on to the next problem.

There are several things that happen due to this behaviour: management teams have to constantly 're-visit' old problems and issues, resulting in eventual fire-fighting when things get out of hand; management and employees are faced with task overload because there is no substantive plan in place to deal effectively with problems, resulting in more things falling through the cracks; and managers and employees lose their motivation and commitment to organization direction, because they sense that there is no one at the helm of the organization making sound decisions.

There are several actions that can be taken to eliminate the problem. First, use a solid planning process that articulates what needs to be done, for what reasons, with appropriate resources, with specific timelines, and with specific responsibilities outlined. In a sound planning process, all goals, initiatives, targets, and activities should track directly to the organizational vision. If any activities do not point towards the vision, they should be revised. In this way, there will be a logical connection between activities and the achievement of the vision.

Second, when plans are developed, identify what some of the unintended consequences are that might be encountered when the plans are implemented. By identifying potential unintended consequences before they occur, many problems can be eliminated before they cause problems.

Third, when the plans are developed, identify and flesh out contingencies for goals and initiatives that may encounter resistance or anticipated (or unanticipated) problems. If contingency plans are not identified prior to them being needed, the organization will waste time and resources.

Fourth, put structures in place to hold managers and employees accountable for doing what they are supposed to be doing, in full, on time. Companies put performance metrics in place for production workers and service deliverers, and they should have performance metrics in place for their own decision-making. If managers know that they will not be held accountable, there will be slippage in their willingness to do what needs to be done on time, if at all.

Fifth, work to build a culture where employees are so committed to the organization that they step up to challenges before anyone has to ask them to. This is where the strongest leverage resides to eliminate the recurring problem of things not getting done. If the organization has a culture that supports getting things done on time and in full, problems can be avoided. Of course, the only way to build and sustain this type of culture is to have your senior managers model it for the rest of the organization. If the rest of the organization sees that key decisions are not being taken, there will be no incentive for them to do it as well.

To pull all these actions together, it is crucial that managers need to learn how to prioritize what needs to be done. With or without a plan, activities need to be prioritized to avoid task overload. The identification of potential unintended conse-quences needs to include prioritization to ensure that the man-agement can deal effectively with the possible problems that can cause the most devastation to organizational effectiveness. Likewise, contingency plans need to be prioritized to identify potentially needed resources. Without prioritization of activ-ities, it will be virtually impossible to hold managers account-able for doing what is most important. The ability to prioritize, and hold employees and managers accountable for those activi-ties sends a signal that the organization is serious about getting things done, and additionally sends the signal that all employees will be treated the same – a major positive impact on improving an organizational culture.

The real key to getting things done is to learn to prioritize what is most important. So, do you want to start to do this today, or are you too busy right now? With luck, someone else will prob-ably do it so why should you worry?

Questions

- Do things get done in your organization? Are they done on time and in full?
- If they don't, why not?
- Are there contingency plans in case there are problems achieving on-time, in-full completion?
- Have the initiatives, prior to their implementation, been tested to see if the timelines are appropriate and there are adequate resources for completion on time and in full?
- What happens when they are not completed on time and in full?
- What does this do to organizational stress?
- What could this stress lead to?

Realizing the potential of teams

Enabling teams to do what they should be able to do

I recently received a note that expressed the concern of many business leaders. It said 'What do I do when my senior team doesn't gel into a team?' A fair question, and one that does apply to many companies today. In most cases, the heads of companies try to surround themselves with highly effective, completely committed teams of people who will be able to follow the direction set forward by the boss. Good thinking on the boss's part, after all, he or she can't do it all. But after a while, the boss sees that things just aren't getting done, or at very minimum, not done fast enough. He can't understand it; the team is a great team. Every member of the team was picked because of the specific skills they had and the energy they had. The answer is that there is no team in place.

Many management teams are in reality, just a great group of mostly well-intentioned people who have been pulled together to do something. But just by trying really hard, attending all the team meetings and believing that they communicate pretty well does not make them a team. A team – think sports team here – is a group of people who all see a common vision and are dedicated to attaining that vision . . . collectively. This can mean that whilst one person on the team may be more visible than the rest, they all work together to make sure they accomplish what they set out to accomplish. In business, this may mean that they not only satisfy all the boss's wishes for their departments, but they do it in the *context* of the overall organization. In short, a team in a business context is a group of well-intentioned people who behave like a team, putting individual and departmental goals and political agendas secondary to a company's vision and its ability to achieve it.

To enable teams to act like teams, there are several things that you will need to do.

1   Ensure that the team has a common view of where the business is going, and how it is going to get there. There are many ways to accomplish this, but one method that works extremely well is to put all the team members in a room and take them through an exercise where they describe how they see the various elements of organizational success, both now and in the future. These elements include: the 'vision' (if the entire company were in one room, what would you see if you looked in the window?); the 'mental models' of the managers and employees (what beliefs and assumptions about the organization do they hold/will they need to hold); the organizational 'structures' (these include the policies and procedures that the company operates under, both implicit and explicit); the 'patterns of behaviour' that management, customers, and suppliers would be able to see; and the 'events' that will be highly visible (that might include profits, revenues, head counts, etc.). When they have all filled in a matrix with these elements listed on it, they would share their work with their team members, giving insights as to how they see their organizational world. This exercise is a very powerful way to ensure a common view for all the team members.

2   Ensure that the team members clearly see how each of their roles contribute to the overall organizational direction. In some organizations I have seen, there are two clearly evident levels of team participation; those team members that do the real work of the company, and those other guys who sit in the offices of a human resources or marketing department. True, it is the operators of any business who are out on the front-lines doing the 'work' of the company, but their contributions would go no place without people to do the work who have the right skills, or an outlet for the company's products or services. A good team management team structure is usually comprised of key representatives from each of the company's key processes. Without any one of the key processes, the overall company efforts will not function effectively. Ensuring that each function is represented goes a long way to team members seeing how their contributions lead to overall success, and this would most probably be reflected in the outputs from the previously mentioned exercise.

3 Ensure that team members work collectively. In many cases, team members tend to degenerate into 'strong' and 'weak' participant members, usually based on personality issues. To offset this potentially disastrous dynamic, allow for dedicated time for the team members to talk openly about how they interact. Having an external facilitator might be a good thing for this as quite often the conversation can turn into defensive mode, which is not conducive for any team activities. If team members are going to function collectively as a team, they will need to feel that they can contribute, and that their contributions will be accepted by all (which is not to say that all contributions are the best, only that team members should feel that they *can* contribute).

4 Ensure that when success occurs, it is the team that is rewarded. The real signal to a team that they are recognized as a team is when the entire team is rewarded for success. If they are not rewarded as a team, the signal is that they are not expected to act as a team . . . and then they won't.

The philosophy behind using teams in business is that, if done well, the synergy that can be obtained through teamwork is more powerful than the sum of the parts. But if you aren't seeing your team acting like a team, before you get all crazy, think about what you are doing to send the right signals for team behaviour to them.

Questions

- Does your organization use teams? Are they effective? How do you know?
- What could be done to make them more effective?
- Does your organization reward teams for performance or individuals?
- Are the teams in your organization realizing their potential?
- What could be done to enable them to do so?

One from column A and one from column B?

Getting your structure right the first time

How do you suppose many organizational structures come about? Here are your choices: (a) a planning group works diligently to determine which structure is most appropriate for the business?; (b) a planning group works diligently to determine which structure is most appropriate for the business strategy?; (c) a planning group works diligently to determine which structure makes sense for the marketplace?; (d) it evolved over time. If you picked 'd', you are right. Yes, many organizations have worked really hard to match a structure where the organization is trying to go, but believing and doing are two different things.

Many organizational structures, much like all living things on this planet, have evolved over time. And because of this evolutionary process, rarely do we even feel the process occurring. And then one day we go to work and notice that there is a clear mismatch between the structure that exists, and the structure that is most appropriate and needed to ensure that the company has a chance to realize its potential.

When this happens – when you realize that the organizational structure doesn't match with the structure that is needed – you have two options. Option one is to tinker with the existing structure. Tinkering with an organizational structure is like ordering from a Chinese menu and saying, 'I'll have some of that and some of that', and about as effective as putting posh-looking seat covers on a Citroën 2CV and expecting that your car will now magically be a 7-Series BMW. Option two is to determine what structure is really needed, and then bite the bullet and change what you have so it is what you need. Matching an organizational structure so it can meet your needs is not easy work. But if you are serious about having a structure that will enable the company to realize its potential, you have little choice. Here is how to do it.

First, you need to have a clear picture of both why the company exists (its mission) and what you are trying to achieve in the company (its vision for the future). Too often, the stated mission and vision of a company are just trendy, well written words cranked out by some marketing staff people, but really don't reflect the reality of the situation, and even worse, are not clearly understood by the managers and employees. Clarity around mission and vision are key, because without them, it is hard to conceive how managers and employees will be able to see how their efforts actually contribute to organizational success.

Second, a structure needs to be designed and tested to ensure that it actually does support the processes and systems of the company. Testing an organizational structure is a bit more than just typing it up on a set of slides. Will the new structure reduce duplication in processes and systems; will it reduce the variation in the way the work is actually done; and will it result in increased effectiveness? An efficient structure is nice, but it may not be the best.

Third, you need to ensure that you have a structure that delivers the right amount of horsepower to ensure growth, and sustain that growth. The whole issue of 'horsepower' is extremely important, as many organizations are able to deliver results on a sporadic basis, but over time, this ability is diluted by reactive thinking, fire-fighting, and organizational malaise. The 'right' structure is one that drives performance, but does so by appropriate technological investments and equally important investments in people. If you aren't able to (or don't choose to) invest in your own future, you will never be able to realize your potential, because your competitors are doing it every day. You need the horsepower to be on the same pitch so you can play the game.

Fourth, you need to ensure that you have the right people in the right jobs. The whole issue of the right people in the right jobs involves looking at what competencies are needed to do specific jobs and then comparing them with what competencies your people have currently. And the comparison needs to go far deeper than making sure that managers have the appropriate technical skills. All managers need to have high levels of people skills – being a good manager means that you need to be able to communicate and enlist the support of those you manage. The very bottom line of management competencies is that managers need to have high levels of abilities to address the challenges they face, gain support for initiatives, get the job done, and do it collectively. In short, these competencies are thinking, influencing, achieving and leading. Regardless of whether managers are in finance, HR, operations, maintenance, sales, or any other business function; they need to be competent in these areas. If you don't have the right people in the right jobs, move them out and get the right people in. If you don't, you will continually be fighting an uphill battle.

The challenge of designing an organizational structure that can enable your company to realize its potential should not be underestimated. Unless of course, you are content with getting the results you have been getting.

Questions

• Do you know what your organizational structure is? Not just the hierarchical chart, but the way that business is conducted?

- If you don't, how can you find out?
- Do you believe that there is a high level of alignment around the understanding of the structure?
- Is the existing structure as effective as it could be to satisfy the organization mission and vision?
- Will this structure enable your organization to realize its potential, or will it result in future chaos and crisis?

Orderly transitions

Avoiding setting yourself up for a crisis

We all know the saying, 'the King is dead; long live the King'. But in the world of business, the saying today might be more like, 'the CEO is gone, long rule the CEO'; or perhaps even, 'the CEO is going to jail, who will be clean enough to take his place?' Hopefully, the latter is not the one that most companies are reciting nowadays.

The ability of a company to have an orderly transition from one leader to the next can impact an organization in many ways. Many new business leaders feel the need to 'make their mark' on their new company, and because the average tenure for CEOs seems to keep falling, they feel the need to do it quickly. Quite often, that means changing corporate direction. These changes can be slight or major, but by putting their mark on the company by flexing their CEO-power, they are able to make sure that their time in the posh office is recognized. And recognized it is, but there can be a downside to this.

Managerial and employee alignment tends to slip away when corporate direction is changed. Not surprisingly, this is an outcome of the fact that changes are rarely communicated as clearly as the boss sees them. For many managers and employees, the messages are received only partially, or at very minimum, only partially understood. And when either of these occurs, the tendency is to fill in the blanks with what we *think* or what we would *like to think*. The outcome of this is misapplied efforts, misapplied resources, and mistakes in decision-making. Getting back to where things should be (or need to be) can be a painful and costly experience. And with this pain comes a reduced ability to meet the needs of customers – something that no business can afford to let happen.

Organization culture can take a serious hit when a new CEO comes onboard. I know of an organization that brought in a new

CEO to fix the mess left by the previous one, and in the first management meeting, the new guy decided he was going to set the stage for big changes – changes that needed to be made. But what he was going to do wasn't the problem; it was the way he said it. Within less than 30 minutes, the organizational climate went from extremely low numbers to flat out zero. The managers became almost paranoid about doing anything that might be construed by the new guy as a signal that they weren't team players, or even worse, as incompetent. Any progress in the company screeched to a halt and fear reigned for several months. Yes, some of the people were probably not competent to manage, but the CEO's comments drove even the competent ones to ground.

When things like alignment and culture are negatively impacted, the chances of sustaining gains in the area of performance suffer. And when performance suffers, this pain is transferred immediately to customers. Customers who become concerned about new leadership tend to begin to look elsewhere for goods and services, and then the problems only escalate.

When a new CEO is so busy flitting about, making himself (or herself) visible to the organization and trying to sort out the myriad of problems that they face, they aren't able to do the job they were hired to do. The new job description becomes one centred on damage control – not a good environment for managers, employees and customers alike. And over time, the Board gets a sense of all the unrest and chaos and does what most Boards do; they decide to make another change in the front office. And the cycle continues.

Some companies (and CEOs) do survive, however. I know of one who has done a brilliant job of putting his mark on the company, building alignment, and increasing organizational culture, all at the same time. But to do it, he spends most of his time on the road. On the surface, this might seem like a good thing. His company is clicking along like a well-made watch. But for the past several years, because he is so busy doing what he does best, he has not taken any time to do any succession planning.

One of the key responsibilities for any competent CEO is to make sure that if he decides to leave (either voluntarily or otherwise), the company will be postured to ensure that the next transition is orderly. Getting the company to run well is important; creating an environment in which it can continue, long after a change in the head office, is critical.

Questions

- Does your organization have a succession-planning process in place in order to avoid the crises that can occur with management changes?
- Does it use it?
- Does the process apply for all levels of the organization? If not, why not?

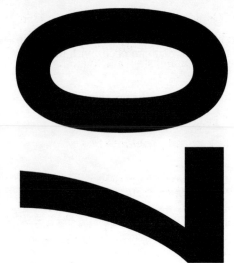

07

finding out what we don't know

In this chapter you will learn:

- how to make better decisions
- how to know what to watch for
- how to leverage structures for success

Surviving change and avoiding crises can be problematic in organizations where there are serious information gaps. But even worse is when organizations don't even know what they don't know. This can make survival an uphill slog, and avoiding crises a virtual impossibility.

Knowing what we don't know

Changing the way we think about problems and challenges

One of the key stumbling blocks that businesses seem to trip over is the ability to know what to do for their customers. Oh yes, we *think* we know because we do surveys that are supposed to tell us what types of services or products customers want, but is that all? Or are we simply falling into the trap of hearing the words, but missing what is behind them?

I recently spent quite a bit of time talking to the CEO of an SME producer of commercial goods and as part of our conversation, I asked him how he was sure that they *knew what they really needed to know*. His response was what I would expect – 'we hold focus groups with our customers on a regular basis to make sure that we are meeting their needs'. Okay, fair enough. But that implies that the only customers they are concerned with are the ones they currently have. And in today's business world, that is just not enough.

There are only three groups of customers out there: the ones you have who love what you do; the ones who don't think you are doing too well at meeting their needs; *and the ones you don't have yet*. There has certainly been quite a bit of research on the cost of getting new customers vs. the cost of retaining existing ones, and the outcome of this research roughly says that it is far less expensive to keep your current customers than to go find new ones. The implication of this research is that it makes sense to not alienate your customers, because if you do, it will cost far more to replace them. Fair enough again. But too often, this is the only message that registers with corporate decision-makers.

The message is that if you would think of your business in terms of a pie chart, you would be able to see how big a slice of that pie you have, and you need to retain. Because if you don't and your slice decreases in size, it will be costly to get that slice up to the size you want at a later date. But what is missed here is that there is another way to look at the *customer pie*.

If you want to grow your business, instead of just looking to steal parts of other suppliers' pie-slices; why not *expand the pie itself*.

Expanding the pie is not that difficult, but it does require that *what you do* is looked at differently. Recently, I received a phone call from someone who wanted some career advice. He said that he was considering going back to school to get an MBA, largely because in his job search, he had been repeatedly told that, whilst he had appropriate skills, he had little industry knowledge. His question was, 'how do I pick an industry I would like to work in?' I replied that first he needed to understand what each industry really did. Not the obvious description, but what they *really* did.

I wanted him to stretch his thinking, so I asked him about DeBeers, the South African diamond company. 'What does DeBeers do?' I asked. 'That's easy, they mine and sell diamonds and other precious jewels' he replied. The obvious answer. I pressed a bit further; 'but what do they *really* do?' After some thought, he replied, 'they make dreams come true'.

Too often, we believe that because a company has an obvious mission to do one thing, it is trapped in that form of product or service delivery. Years ago, I did some work with a manufacturing company that was not doing well. Their market share was dissipating at a speed that was only equalled by their shrinking bank balance. Instead of helping them to make a bigger presence in the marketplace, I began to get them to explore what else they could produce with their existing equipment, and within short order, they were able to begin producing other products with the same machines . . . and expand their view of *how big their pie could be*. They were able to utilize what they had to do something new that enabled them to access a whole *new pie*.

By shifting our thinking about what we do instead of only looking to increase your slice of the existing business pie, an organization has the ability to expand its customer base, without having to spend excessive amounts trying to take business away from existing competition.

Will this work for all companies? Maybe, maybe not, but unless management decision-makers take the time to think about what they really do, they will be forever stuck in a mental model that can be highly restrictive. And they will spend all their time trying to just get a bigger slice of the pie.

Questions

- Do your decision-makers know what they need to know to ensure long-term, sustainable success?
- Do they know what they don't know?
- Are they making an attempt to find out what they don't know?

How incentives can go wrong

Why incentives can cause more problems than they solve

If there is something that management has figured out, it is to incentivize employees to demonstrate sought after performance behaviours. When you think about it, creating incentives does seem like a rational way to deal with the problem, especially when all the talk in the world may not have made a difference in achieving the outcomes that management might be looking for. Since using the whip went out long ago as a way to convince people to do the 'right thing', the application of incentives may make sense in specific situations. However, in many situations, the people who identify and create the incentive programmes appear to not understand how employees react to the programmes they come up with.

First, employees are not stupid people. Actually, they are quite smart, and after years of listening to management's shifts in internal messages, they have become quite savvy in figuring out ways to make the incentive programmes *appear* to be effective, whilst at the same time, be defeated through the application of *creativity*.

Several years ago, management at a service organization in the US discovered that their procurement people were spending far more than they were budgeted to spend on acquiring products and services. After a year of 'don't do this anymore', and 'hey fellas, let's keep the spending in line with our plans', someone in management made the decision to bring in a consultancy to develop a set of incentives to curtail the excessive spending behaviour. On the surface, this sounded like a good idea, but over time, even with the incentive programme, spending continued to escalate and the consultants were brought back to develop an additional incentive programme. To some, myself included, this seemed to be folly: you have a problem, so you try to resolve it with incentives (that don't appear to work), so then you do more of the same. One shouldn't need to have a PhD in organizational behaviours to see the folly in this type of thinking, but it happened in this organization, and it happens in many other organizations as well.

The situation was this: the procurement people were charged with 'buying' equipment that was incredibly expensive. The suppliers were clearly happy to sell to them, and the procurement people were hitting all their metrics for purchasing. But over time, costs kept increasing faster than budget planners could anticipate the increases and this escalation of costs triggered the management response of retaining the services of a large consultancy with a reputation for incentive programme development and implementation.

The incentive programme was laid out to provide cash incentives for the procurement people every time they could buy the equipment at the cost that was in the budget. With the best of intentions, efforts were made to pressure suppliers to hold the price line, but the suppliers knew that they were in control, as in most cases, the equipment was proprietary and the organization had to deal with them . . . or not have the equipment it needed. Every time one of the procurement personnel contacted a supplier to check current prices, they were told that the price had increased; in many cases by increases of ten to twenty per cent or more. And when this would occur, the staff in procurement were faced with a choice: (a) hold to the organization policy of only purchasing based on planned budgetary costs; (b) don't purchase from this supplier; and (c) figure out a way to keep costs in line with budgets and keep on purchasing. If they opted out for keeping costs in line with budgets, the suppliers wouldn't sell to them – not a good way to keep your job. If they opted out for not purchasing at increased price, they would not be able to purchase, as the suppliers had proprietary equipment that could not be acquired from other sources – again, not a good way to keep your job. So they opted out for the last option, and figured out how to acquire equipment at the pre-planned cost, whilst at the same time, being a recipient of a nice cash incentive. Of course, the way this was accomplished was by 'gaming the system'.

The procurement people (not all of them initially, just the most 'creative') sat down with the suppliers and explained the situation. They wanted to buy equipment; the suppliers wanted to sell; and unless they could figure out a way past the existing system, there was a risk that new suppliers would step into the ever-increasing gap of acceptable suppliers. The success of these 'negotiations' was, of course, complicated a bit by the fact that there were now cash incentives to be had for the procurement staff. What they came up with was a process in which the suppliers would sell the equipment to the organization at preplanned budgeted prices – making the procurement people look good and enable them to receive the cash incentives – but with a little addition. To keep the costs in line with what the organization had budgeted, the suppliers and the procurement people wrote up a set of ongoing 'maintenance' contracts. These contracts more than covered the difference in what the supplier wanted and what the organization wanted to spend. Now one might say that these maintenance contracts, when combined with the purchase price, would exceed the planned costs – which they did – but the metrics that were being applied to the procurement people as a way to measure whether or not they should receive the incentive payments *was only on the purchase price, not the overall cost.*

It took the organization over a year to discover that their overall costs were still escalating way beyond their planned budgets, and then all management did was to bring back the consultants to whip out more incentives. The problem was that the initial incentives were being applied based on the wrong criteria.

Incentive programmes such as the one in this example can be applied at one of three different levels of interpretation. The three levels are, the 'event' level, the 'pattern of behaviour' level, or at the 'structural level'. These three levels represent an iceberg. In an iceberg, there are several 'levels'. There is the tip of the iceberg – the part that is easy to see and recognize; the part just below the surface of the water; and the largest part, the part that is far below the surface. The tip of an iceberg can be equated to the event level in an organization – easy to see and recognize, but seeing the tip of an iceberg really doesn't provide much information on the size or scope of the iceberg, nor does it explain what makes the iceberg move in the way that it does; just as seeing events occurring in an organization does not explain why they happen or how to avoid them in the future. The part of an iceberg just below the surface of the water can be equated to organizational patterns of behaviour – it is constantly changing due to the effects of waves and water currents, just as organizational performance keeps evolving over time. The structural level of an iceberg – the part far below the surface of the water – can provide a wealth of information about why the iceberg is the size it is, why it may move as it does, and why it will react the way it does to external stimuli; just as the structural level of an organization

Figure 15

can be used to understand why employees react the way they do
to various stimuli (such as management incentive programmes).

As can be seen in Figure 15, the event level, or tip of the iceberg
is very easy to see and identify, and yet, just knowing about it
provides very low leverage to understand the iceberg itself, or
what it will do over time. But the structural level (the part that is
far below the surface of the water) is very difficult to see, but can
provide a wealth of information about the iceberg, and what it
will do in the future. This model can be applied to understanding what will happen when programmes such as the incentive
programme in the example are attempted.

Whilst the incentive programme had been developed with the
express intent to achieve better financial outcomes for the organization, the way in which it had been implemented actually *dis-
incentivized* the procurement people to do just that. Instead, they
were incentivized to do whatever they needed to do to hit their
metrics of *purchased equipment at a specific pre-planned cost*.
The fact that their actions caused the organization to actually
expend more money over time didn't feed into the equation,
because of the way the incentives were produced and implemented. And even worse, the procurement people were quite

open about what they were doing – through a series of interviews, it was openly admitted that they were 'gaming the system'.

The two major elements of the incentive programme were: (a) purchase the equipment at a pre-planned price; and (b) the cash incentives. Achieving the pre-planned purchase price is an event – easy to see, easy to recognize. But the cash incentive component of the incentive programme was in reality, a systemic structure element – it dis-incentivized the procurement people to strive for the first programme element. The procurement people who were interviewed openly admitted that the reason that they gamed the system in the way that they did – forcing the organization to pay even more than they had previously – was driven by the chance to receive cash bonuses.

And if that isn't bad enough, the organization in the example was a government agency and even though it knew the folly of what was occurring through the implementation of the incentive programme(s), the agency did nothing to stop it . . . because it was part of government and there was pressure to get the equipment in service.

Questions

- Does your organization use incentive programmes?
- Do your organizational incentive programmes have unintended consequences that have been examined before implementation?
- How do you know if your incentive programmes will achieve the results you are looking for, or will they, in reality, dis-incentivize employees to achieve desired performance behaviours?
- Are the employees who will be targeted by a proposed incentive programme involved in the development of the programme, or are they just subject to its implementation?
- If you have an incentive programme that is not working in the way it was intended, will you change it, or just press on with it further?

The brainstorming debate

Leveraging your potential to avoid problems

In a recent issue of the *Daily Telegraph* (14 July 2005), Professor Heinz Shuler talked about the need for solid, empirically derived data when making business decisions. Well, I would agree . . . to a point. Whilst he is right that empirical research data is extremely important, brainstorming has an extremely beneficial role in the decision-making process. This is especially important in an environment in which change is ever-present, and crises loom on the horizon.

Shuler was quoted as being *'critical of the usual brainstorming sessions that are so common in practice. He stresses that only scientifically conducted empirical studies produce reliable results.'* Okay, fair enough. We all can have our own view, but I think that he is missing the whole point of brainstorming here.

Brainstorming is not just a group of people who are throwing out ideas that have no connection to the reality of a given situation. Brainstorming is a way to obtain valuable input that otherwise would not be available to decision-makers. Too often, managers do not take into consideration the mental models, beliefs and assumptions that other managers and employees hold about the potential for a data-driven initiative to succeed. Data may be great to use to help determine where an organization is today (and therefore to do something different if it is not happy where it is) but all the data in the world, scientifically developed or not, cannot guarantee that the decisions that managers make will turn out the way they want them to. Data cannot chart a path forward, only identify if the organization is on the path that was chosen.

It is the mental models of managers and employees that are best to use for determining *how* to do something best. We all live in our own realities. How many readers think that the guys that were at the helm of MG Rover or some of the other major corporate disasters made the right decisions? At the time, apparently quite a few people did. Data have shown us that they were wrong, but had the management of these companies been open to some brainstormed feedback, they might not have gotten into the mess they found themselves in.

I have interviewed managers and employees of organizations who are quite open about the fact that they do not believe that 'management is competent to lead', and that this or that initiative 'will not go the way' that management wants it to. And in most cases, this is because the managements in question have not listened to, nor asked for, input from the front-line about what works and what doesn't work.

Example: a large service organization that had for many years driven its strategic planning process almost solely based on heavily researched data about competition. The research was quite good, and the company's management had invested heavily in ensuring that it was complete. The research organization that had put it together had done so by looking almost exclusively at published and audited information, which they then put into charts and graphs. The strategies, however, rarely worked. After talking with many employees, it became apparent that the reason they didn't work was because the data missed several key points.

The front-line employees had access to customer information that the researchers didn't have, largely because of their inter-actions, and unfortunately, as they were not part of the strategic development process, this information was never surfaced. And because the front-line was never invited to participate, they (correctly) assumed that their input was not valued by management. This led them to believe that there was little reason for them to contribute and/or be committed to company initiatives. Yes, they were compliant – they followed the 'letter' of the plan, but rarely would extend themselves to make sure that the plans would succeed. This began to set up an adversarial relationship with management that was in existence until senior management was changed and the employees were invited to participate in the planning process.

In the new process, planning sessions include management, unions, non-represented front-line workers, as well as the traditional company planners. And in this process, brainstorming was structured and facilitated, not to supplant the research, but to validate what the research says, and determine the best path forward.

Structured, facilitated brainstorming usually invokes a set of tools that keep the participants focused on the issues at hand. Many of these tools were developed by the Japanese in the 1970s in order to ensure that companies were doing the right things, for the right reasons, and at the right time. The Affinity Process is used to sort out the myriad of ideas that participants have about what needs to be done. An Interrelationship Digraph is a brain-storming tool that is used to determine how to ensure that the return on investment of time and effort when considering an initiative is well placed. An Arachnid Chart helps put clarity around how much effort and/or progress is being made in the implementation of an initiative; and a simple Matrix can help shed light on the various connections between two or more sets of organizational variables (such as Customers' Needs and the ways in which a company sets out to meet them). All these tools use brainstorming, and they can provide incredible leverage for an organization when doing planning. Should they be used without access to hard data? Of course not, but the data only tells the story of 'today'. And through the use of facilitated, structured brainstorming tools, management can more effectively plot the way towards the organizational tomorrow.

'Scientifically conducted empirical studies' are wonderful to have access to, but the bottom line is that all the empirical data in the world won't mean anything if there is no common sense available to do something with it. Brainstorming is a powerful organizational tool. It should not be used in lieu of data, but to help ensure that all that empirically developed research isn't just relegated to the scrap heap of good intentions.

Questions

- Does your organization utilize brainstorming as a way to help solve problems?
- Does the organization utilize (or support the development and training of) trained facilitators to ensure that brainstorming is effective?
- Are the employees encouraged to provide their input to resolve long-standing problems?
- Is that input valued?

Robbing Peter to pay Paul?
Getting a better perspective on it all

Too often, management can become distracted from the implicit challenge that they face. Yes, the explicit challenge is to ensure that the respective organizations that they are responsible for are successful and profitable. But the implicit challenge is to ensure that the decisions they make not only deliver this success next quarter, but in *every* quarter. And to accomplish this, what happens is that they do the equivalent of 'robbing Peter to pay Paul'.

As pressure continues from shareholders and external analysts to 'deliver profits', some managers fall into the behaviour of making short-term decisions, based on reactive thinking. This is really no different from someone who borrows against his or her future salary just to keep food on the table. Eventually, this behaviour catches up to the borrower. And just as it catches up to us as individuals, it will catch up to businesses as well. Eventually, there will be nothing left from future potential earnings to 'borrow' from, and then the end is near. This doesn't need to happen; but to avoid it, it requires two things: a shift in thinking that borrowing from the future is okay; and, a clear understanding of what the unintended consequences of these actions are.

Whilst talking to a senior manager of a large manufacturing company recently, it became clear that 'robbing Peter to pay Paul' was not only accepted in his organization, it was rewarded. It was common knowledge that when the sales unit of the company was not 'hitting their numbers', the sales managers were clearly told that they had 'better make sure that the targets were achieved, or else'. The message of 'or else' was a pretty clear signal that their jobs were at risk. So what would you do in that situation? The tendency is to start counting 'possibles' as real sales, or keep discounting until the customer agreed to place an order. Each of these behaviours has major unintended consequences.

Counting future sales as existing sales keeps the cycle of 'robbing Peter to pay Paul' alive and forces sales people to stay locked into this vicious cycle. Deep discounting causes additional shortfalls in financial terms, with the end result being more pressure to produce. Again, reinforcing this very vicious cycle. And the problem does not appear solely in the sales area. Quite often, we have seen production areas under extreme pressure to run at higher than rational levels, just to 'hit the numbers' that have been targeted. In many cases, this results in bypassing required maintenance. It is like driving your car at full speed 24 hours per day, day after day, with the hope that you will get further down the road than your competitor. But we know that if you do not stop to re-fuel or do prescribed maintenance, the car will simply cease to run at some point, and then your competitor will simply cruise past you.

This is an issue about organizational performance. And if achieving high performance isn't complex enough, in today's business world, you must be able to continually improve on your performance.

Here is the priority hierarchy of performance: (a) be able to 'hit the numbers'; (b) be able to hit higher and higher numbers; (c) be able to demonstrate the ability to hit higher and higher numbers, consistently. Just being able to do 'a' is simply not good enough anymore, nor is being able to do 'b'. The ability to demonstrate hitting higher and higher numbers consistently is the real challenge.

Organizations need to ensure that they have in place, a solid structure and culture that fosters continual performance improvement, and they need to do it through a clear demonstration of leadership. Traditional management just won't cut it anymore. You can't 'manage' your way out of a structure and culture that propagates 'robbing Peter to pay Paul'.

What is required is a solid grounding in the key elements of sustainable performance improvement. These elements include: a clearly visible and understandable strategic vision for the future; an organizational structure, business processes, and human resource architecture that are in alignment with the vision; support and commitment to the ongoing application of technological innovation; and an organizational culture that accepts and is committed to achieving the vision. And the only way that these elements can take hold in an organization is through clear, committed, visible leadership.

Now many organizational decision-makers would say that they do have these elements in place; but the reality is that if they were, and even more importantly, the way in which these elements interacted with each other were solidly in place, the performance-based behaviour of 'robbing Peter to pay Paul' would not occur. This is a greater issue than how best to cut costs; this is a greater issue than just how to get things done; this is an issue about choice. And the choice is, 'do we want our organizations to be able to consistently deliver high performance and realize their potential?' If the answer is 'yes', then the management needs to make a choice to that effect. Would implementing this choice be difficult? Perhaps. But the reality is that management is paid to make tough choices, and this decision is far more beneficial over time than just about any other decision that could be made.

Questions

- Do the management of your organization understand the challenges they face?
- Do they communicate these challenges, and what they plan to do about them, to the organization as a whole?

- Are they competent to lead the organization, or are they just good managers?
- How do they deal with change and the potential for crises?
- If a major crisis would occur, would they be able to lead the organization away from it? Would their solution be sustainable?

133
finding out what we
don't know

07

The perfect storm of impending crisis

**When everything goes wrong at once,
and we miss the signals**

As with most organizations, problems, or perhaps more appropriately potential problems, do not appear on their own. Most problems are connected to other problems, and by trying to solve only one of them can exacerbate the other ones. And yet, trying to attack them all at the same time rarely yields good results. This could be due to the fact that many problem solvers apparently don't see the interconnections, or it could be a lack of energy to go after them all, or it even could be because the expectation of solving them all is so low that problem solvers are implicitly told to just do what you can and get back to doing the day job. I tend to think the reason that the problems don't completely go away is a little of each reason, but largely because the interconnections can be difficult to see, especially in organizations that have fixed problem-solving processes that do not delve deep enough.

I received an email from a friend with a set of stories from the same organization that were all interconnected. The stories all represented ongoing problems for the company – problems that seemed to be unsolvable and were coming together as if it were the 'perfect storm' of business problems.

The story takes place in a multinational manufacturing company. Note that the identifier of 'multinational' alludes to the potential for both real and perceived complexity. The company has patents on a variety of its products, patents that are based on the intellectual property of the organization, and because of that, have considerable value.

Problem element 1: At one point, one of the senior decision-makers of one of the company's divisions (for the purposes of the story, division A) decided to allow a competitor to license the manufacture of one of the patented products. For a variety of reasons, this seemed to be a good idea at the time; the division wasn't in a position to do an effective marketing of the product but knew that it was marketable, as it had substantial product intellectual property value. Licensing a competitor to produce the product was a good strategy to get extra value out of it, and at the same time, helped to offset additional research investment being spent on new products.

However, when the news began to leak out internally of the decision, the heads of division B became frustrated and incensed. They felt that they were both eager and postured appropriately to market the product themselves. Their logic made sense too. They had access to the same market the competitor had; they had the resources to do an effective job of marketing; and they were in the same corporate structure. They were mystified why the guys in division A would license a competitor to market a product that they could have marketed, effectively being able to increase corporate contributions.

Problem element 2: Division B has a product that they have developed and hold a patent on that they have been marketing for some time, however, as the patent protection approaches its expiration, one of the senior decision-makers in division A grants a licence for a competitor to market the product under the competitor's name. On the surface once again, this could be interpreted as a sound business decision, as all revenues at one point or another flow into the corporate accounts.

Problem element 3: Division A has been undergoing a cost-reduction programme and one of the outcomes of the effort has been the identification of 'surplus' equipment and facilities and commitments. So, as a result of the cost-cutting effort, the decision was made to close down one of their manufacturing sites. In order to not have this decision negatively impact customers, the decision included a plan to outsource the products that were previously being manufactured at the site. Sound thinking some would say – the site is expensive to operate so close it, but to avoid disrupting production, outsource the manufacturing operations. Production (and revenues) continues whilst expenses are reduced. However, as the plan was communicated, it becomes apparent that division B, which had excess capacity in their facilities, expresses their concerns that they were not given the opportunity to take over production. When this was discussed in a decision-making meeting, one of the managers from division A was heard to say that, *'we don't trust these guys'*, referring to some of the personnel in division B.

Problem element 4: The head of the business sector, whilst quite competent in driving his sector's business apparently is not as competent in finances. This surfaces in a meeting where it becomes clear that he doesn't fully understand how to calculate his sector's return on sales efforts. His understanding was that sales between divisions actually reduces financial results due to high internal profit margins set for the various divisions.

These stories demonstrate a series of individual, but interconnected problems. Due to the fact that the multinational company had been structured to have separate divisions that were run autonomously, the problems appeared to be isolated. And because of this, they represented just the tip of the iceberg. Clearly, as these problems escalated (which they had been doing over time), the company was fast approaching a crisis point – how to ensure that the differing perceptions of divisional decision-makers did not negatively impact long-term corporate profits. The perfect storm of problems was about to erupt.

The problems listed were in reality, just symptoms of a greater set of problems. These included lack of alignment in overall organizational goals; lack of understanding of organizational strategies; excessively poor inter-divisional communications; lack of problem-solving skills; and a clearly depressed competence in the ability to recognize the interrelationship of divisional issues.

In problem element 1, the decision to license a corporate competitor to manufacture a product was good, based on the situation division A was in. However, by making this decision arbitrarily, an unintended consequence was the alienation of a different corporate division.

In problem element 2, the decision on the part of division A to license a product with a short patent protection life to a different competitor again makes sense; but only with a myopic view of the overall corporate structure. The fact that the product was, at the time, manufactured by a different internal division (division B) resulted in the unintended consequence of further alienating a sister organization.

In problem element 3, the decision by division A to reduce costs by closing a site and outsource the manufacturing processes of that site can, and should be, interpreted to be sound and rational. However, without exploring other internal options for the manufacture of corporately-owned products, this decision becomes myopic and open to re-assessment. The fact that a manager from division A was overheard stating that 'we don't trust' the other division (B) can lead one to question the validity of the actual decision-making process that was used.

And in problem element 4, the financial competence level of an extremely senior person aggravated the first three problem elements. The matter of leadership competence – in this case, management competence as from the story, it is pretty clear that the sector man is not demonstrating leadership behaviours – has both a direct and indirect impact on organizational effectiveness. The direct impact manifests itself in the performance of the organization, or in this case, the various divisions in his sector. The indirect impact manifests itself in the behaviours of the people within, in this case, the sectors.

This company has a problem, and from the interviews, it is clear that they don't even understand how close they are to a major crisis. If they want to avoid the crisis from rearing its head, there are several things that can be done.

Due to the various elements of their problem, they need to:

1 Convene meetings with divisional leaders expressly for the purpose of surfacing mental models about how they see their interrelationships with other divisional decision-makers. It is clear from the comments overheard about low levels of trust between divisions, that until existing mental models can be surfaced and dealt with, there will always be problems in creating an environment in which the overall organization will be able to realize its potential. These sessions will need to be facilitated, as the conversation may be quite testy, as it can be when talking about trust. The objective of such meetings would not necessarily be to instil trust initially, but instead to create an environment in which trust can be demonstrated and trustworthiness can be earned.

2 Change the way decisions that could possibly impact other organization divisions are made. Currently, it is clear that each division operates autonomously, which can be good, except in situations where one division's decisions can negatively impact the potential of another. The context is, of course, that all the divisions are part of one organization, and the bottom line is *organizational success, not simply divisional success*. This process should undoubtedly be led by the sector head, with decisions being tested before they are implemented. In this type of process of testing decisions, it can be very beneficial to continually ask the questions, 'if we do this, what will we get? And then what else may we get?' If the response to the latter question is, 'not sure', then the meeting leader should say, 'think harder'. For every action (decision), there is a reaction, and finding out what the reactions will be before they occur can eliminate the potential for serious problems later. The objective is to both help decision-makers think more systemically, and to help them have a better understanding of the organizational impacts of their decision-making process.

3   Ensure that the organization has the right people in the right jobs, for the right reasons, with the right skills. Having demonstrable technical skills is extremely important, but ensuring that managers (like in the case of the sector manager) have high levels of interpersonal skills can be brutally critical. Whilst the existing sector manager seems to have a gap in his financial thinking and understanding, the more critical gap is shown by the fact that the decision-makers in the divisions that supply the products he is responsible for don't communicate, nor do they trust each other enough to even attempt communications. Not having the right people, with the right skills in critical positions can generate crisis as much as not having customers or products to sell them.

The problems being experienced within the organization are not unique. Too many companies suffer from the same or similar dynamics, and as a result, can end up on the edge of crisis, as is seen in the story. The ability to get through them is a choice; but the effort will require a serious commitment to the overall organization. And at the end of the day, creating an environment in which an organization can realize its potential does seem to be the most important factor in deciding to change how decisions are made.

Questions

- Is there trust in your organization? How do you know?
- Do decision-makers of internally competing business units talk to each other?
- Do they test decisions before they are implemented?
- Are the decision-makers willing to change their decision-making behaviours if it would help the company?
- How can they do this best in your organization?

08

being competent to survive it all

In this chapter you will learn:

- how to build alignment for change
- how to increase your ability to be effective
- how to avoid the plague of stress
- how to see unintended consequences before they cause problems

Making sure that change and crises do not paralyse an organization is common sense. Ensuring that your people have the stalls to do so should be mandatory, for if it is not, the risks of calamity grow quickly.

Understanding alignment gaps

Reducing the potential for crises occurring

In many organizations, getting people onboard to specific change initiatives can be difficult. Part of this is because organizations, for some reason, try to classify initiatives as 'change initiatives' or 'other initiatives', but the reality is that the entire purpose of any initiative is to change the way some things are done. Getting people onboard, on the surface, implies that the people are not onboard, but where many efforts fail is because management really doesn't understand where they actually are. If not 'onboard', are they at least close to being onboard? Are they not onboard because they don't understand why the organization is trying to implement a new way of doing work, or are they not onboard because they dislike the initiative (or the effort to implement it) and will probably crank up their defence mechanisms to resist it? Different mindsets on the part of those onboard require different approaches, but until you actually know, just about anything you do will result in wasted time and resources.

Whilst there has been extensive research done to classify the different types of alignment (or non-alignment) population groups, the bottom line is that there are really only four groups of people worth talking about. These four groups of people can be called, those who understand the initiative and the reasons behind it, those who are highly supportive and buy-in to the effort to implement change, those who are resistant to any change and will probably do what they can to stop the efforts, and those who simply don't 'get it'. By plotting various population groups on a simple 2 × 2 matrix, it is possible to have a good view of how massive the challenge will be to implement change.

Using the matrix template shown in Figure 16 with the four groups identified on opposite axes, it is possible to actually plot out your organizational alignment potential. Note that the actual wording applied to the matrix axes are quite simple and to the point: employees either 'buy-in', they 'understand', they are 'resistant', or they have 'no clue'. There is no reason to use

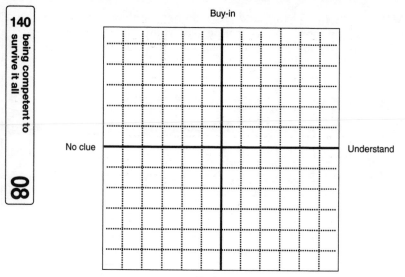

Figure 16

complicated terminology when using this matrix – short, direct, and to the point is common sense.

An actual example of what the output of an alignment matrix might look like is shown in Figure 17. In this actual organizational output, based on work done with a mid-sized service organization with unions, it is possible to see that there is a substantial gap in alignment, and the completed matrix enabled the implementation team to develop a plan to close the gap, based on where the actual gaps were.

This matrix graphically shows the various levels of alignment in three different leadership groups within the same organization. The groups include senior executive management (black circles), the actual change initiative group (white circles), and union leadership (squares). As can be seen, there is little alignment in either the senior executive management team or the change initiative group. The only population group that is currently demonstrating alignment is the union leadership team, and that alignment is manifesting itself as people who have not been told clearly what the initiative is all about, and why it is contemplated.

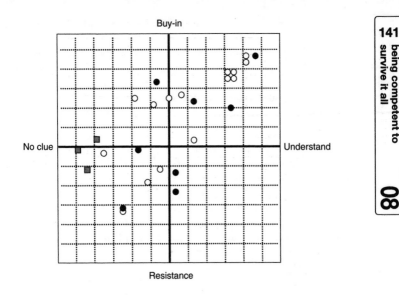

Figure 17

141
being competent to
survive it all

08

Several things stand out dramatically. Of major concern should be the seemingly inconsistencies between the senior executive team members, as well as the same level of understanding and commitment on the part of the actual change initiative group. This will result over time in wasted time, wasted resources, wasted opportunities, and clearly, in an environment of change, the distinct possibility that a *positive, proactive effort* will end up being a forcefully driven effort if at all.

There are things that can be discerned from the matrix that should be done. First, the change initiative team needs to sit down together and bring to the surface what the varying perceptions are amongst the group – if the change group itself is not together, there is no chance that the initiative will work.

Second, the change group needs to meet with the senior management team to build alignment around the rationale behind, and the purpose for, the initiative itself. Due to the fact that most organizations are hierarchical, it would make sense to have this meeting (or meetings) facilitated with someone outside the issue. This could mean using a trained facilitator from another part of the organization, or, if the organization does not have serious, hard-core facilitators in its ranks, using someone from outside the company. Building alignment means surfacing existing mental models about the validity of change initiatives and what can occur if they are not coordinated effectively. But it also means facilitating conversations targeted at helping an organizational population clearly understand that the company will keep changing regardless if there is a structured process to guide it or not. And if there is no guided change process, one day the company may find itself looming over the precipice of non-existence.

Third, it is clear from the matrix that for some reason, senior union personnel have been left out of the communication process. This could have been an oversight, or it could have been intentional (based on the belief that beginning the initiative is a management decision solely). The bottom line is that in most organizations, it is the unionized people who do the real front-line work of the company, and if their senior team is not onboard with any type of initiative, it will be an uphill slog . . . or a complete waste of time and effort.

A good process might look like:

1 build alignment within the change initiative group
2 build alignment within the senior management group
3 get the union leadership onboard
4 hold a meeting with all three population groups to further build and confirm alignment about what will occur, when it will occur, why it will occur, and what success will look like after the initiative is going forward. Part of this would be to have the collective group identify appropriate milestones that can be hit whilst the initiative is in progress, as well as identifying what resources will be needed to ensure success, and what success will look like.

The real message that can be determined from using the matrix is that it can show how much alignment there is, and where the alignment gaps are. If you don't know where the gaps are, there is no way to close them; and if you don't have alignment, everything becomes excessively hard work. Which in today's business world, doesn't make any sense at all.

Questions

- Is there an acceptable level of alignment on the senior management level of your organization? At the mid-management level? On your team level?
- Is the current level of alignment resulting in wasted time and misdirected efforts?

143
being competent to
survive it all

08

- What is the cost of this?
- What is being done to improve alignment; in thinking, in motivation, in strategic direction, in willingness and ability to change, in capacity to avoid crises?

Dealing with stress in the workplace

Making sure that stress doesn't result in additional problems

In *Trendwatcher* (2 September 2005) there was an article titled 'Stressed' that dug into some of the problems that businesses face due to stressed workers. To quote an excerpt from the article, ' *"Burnout happens to highly motivated and committed people . . . There is a connection between idealistic dedication to a job and a heightened tendency to burnout" (Stanley, 2004). Still, many employees are sceptical that management truly cares about the issue. In fact, 71% of 2,500 respondents to a UK survey by the law firm Peninsula say they think their employer doesn't take stress seriously.'* Perhaps they should, and even more importantly, perhaps they should do something about it.

It is pretty sad that, according to the article, burnout plagues those employees who are highly motivated and committed. But it is this very statement that caused me to wonder, *'why would those employees who are highly motivated and committed suffer from stress?'* I could understand it I suppose if stress was rampant in those who were not motivated or committed, after all, wouldn't they be the most concerned about potentially losing their jobs? But then it became clear; perhaps these people aren't stressed because they just don't care. The reason that highly motivated and committed people are stressed is because they do care, and aren't able to get as much done as they would like to get done to help the organization. Admittedly, I don't have piles of empirical data to back up this assertion, but I do have a plethora of interviews with employees who complain that their organizations handcuff them and throw roadblock upon roadblock in front of their efforts to ensure that the company achieves some of its strategic goals.

When digging deeper into these statements, I have found that there are several complaints that stand out.

1 Employees do not have the skills needed to do the jobs that are expected of them.

2 Quite often, budget commitments are slashed once programmes are begun.
3 The idea of 'teamwork' between departments is about as real
as Santa Claus coming down your chimney.
4 Management is so busy coming up with new initiatives that
they rarely allow ones that have begun to complete on time,
in full.

Interestingly enough, when I talk to senior managers about
employee competence, I find a similar list.

1 Many employees do not have the right skills.
2 Budget constraints can be crippling.
3 Employees need to work collectively to get better results.
4 Initiatives are not completed when they need to be completed.

So what is really going on here? If the employee list is relatively
representative of what is happening in many organizations, it is
no wonder that employees (especially those that are highly
motivated and committed) are stressed. And if the managerial
input is somewhat representative, it makes sense why the stress
levels are increasing. In many organizations, when managers
have beliefs about employee competence as the list above shows,
what do you suppose they do? The number of managers that
decide to increase training, lock in budgets, demonstrate teamwork, and stop driving new initiatives until the old ones are fin-
ished could be counted on one hand. Instead, what they do is
crank on the pressure for results. Being told to simply 'work
harder' is not the solution to fundamentally systemic problems.

Management (and I use the term collectively here) needs to figure
out what is most important; getting the job done today, or
making sure that the workforce can get all the jobs done, all the
time, on time, and in full. Granted, with the pervasive amount of
short-term, reactive thinking that is polluting the world of business, it is no wonder that 'getting the job done today' is the
'policy-du-jour'. But hang on for a minute; it is exactly this type
of thinking that has got businesses into some of the messes they
are in.

The heads of the companies in trouble need to take a deep breath
and change their behaviours. They need to ensure that all
employees *do have the skills that they need*. And the first place
to start is to make sure that managers have the right set of interpersonal skills to ensure that more employees can become motivated and committed to organizational goals and targets. Next,

they need to ensure that training is a priority, and that it doesn't fall victim to cost pressures that will arise off and on. Training for all employees, at all levels, is crucial to long-term, sustainable success.

Budgets are put together for a purpose, and if budget managers believe that they will be cut all the time, they will simply game the system and up their requests. Smart thinking actually, if you think your budget will be cut by 10 per cent, up the estimate by 10 per cent when you put the request in. But the finance lads aren't exactly stupid either, and if they think that this form of gaming the system is going on, they will lop off another 10 per cent. Playing this game can be interesting, but it is just a waste of time and resources that could be applied to making sure that the right amount of funds are available to achieve their purpose. Slashing budgets as an ongoing management practice just reflects poor management practice . . . and competence.

Most employees would love to practise teamwork, but in many companies I have spoken with, the structure that they are faced with is set up to foster adversarial 'win–lose' thinking. Providing support, whether intellectual or budgetary, for another department only penalizes your department, why would you want to function as a team? Most reward policies today are geared to identifying 'people' in the singular sense for success, and not for 'people' in the collective sense (think 'employee of the year' or 'sales guy of the month'). And even worse, if you stood to win one of these 'rewards' would you be interested in sharing your glory with everyone who supported your work? Maybe, but usually not. Companies promote people (again, in the singular sense), not teams. This implicit policy does nothing more than exacerbate the entire teamwork dilemma and promote adversarial work relationships within the workforce.

And then there is the issue of 'non-completion'. I can't tell you how often I have seen this dynamic in action. Initiatives are begun with a flourish, but after a while, interest begins to fade and eventually, the only people who are still working on it are those whose jobs are assigned to it. Other employees who were initially assigned to the initiative have been pulled to work on something else, or have managed to make themselves invisible. If management wants to make sure that initiatives are started and completed on time, and in full, they need to first make sure that the initiative is the right thing to do, for the right reasons, at the right time, and with the right resources. Then management needs to demonstrate the same level of commitment to the initiative that they expect from the employees; and finally, management needs to create an environment in which the work can actually get done. Of course, there are some people who don't even have the option to be completers or non-completers. They are told that extra piece of work must get done. We all know how this works; you work all day on the big initiative, then after work, you work all night to try to catch up on the day job responsibilities.

Highly motivated and committed employees stressed out at your company? Well if I worked there under these conditions, I would be too. If management really wants to get more out of their employees, the first thing they should do is look into a mirror and see what they might be doing to contribute to the situation they are in.

Management steps to reduce stress of employees (and increase effectiveness) include:

1   Examine their own behaviours to see if they are contributing to the stress (and low effectiveness) level in the organization. The actions of senior managers are seen by employees, and emulated by mid-managers. If these actions are not congruent with effectiveness, they will demoralize employees who will (correctly) assume that management as a whole operates under a '*do as I say, not as I do*' philosophy.

2   Talk to employees to find out if they see your demonstrated behaviours as conducive to organizational effectiveness, or organizational stress. Conversations such as these need to be non-threatening, and the best way to do this is to explain that your main concern as a manager is to create an environment in which employees can do what they are expected to do. Listen to what they say, and why they say it.

3   Find out if your employees have the skills they need to get their respective jobs done, on time, in full. A good indicator can be found through two questions. Are planned training programmes cancelled or run as scheduled? And, when employees complete training programmes, have their skills really improved? If courses are cancelled, for any reason, you need to begin to think longer term. Ensuring that employees have appropriate skills is the only way to ensure a long-term future for your organization. If skill training doesn't actually improve skills, get a training programme and trainers who know what they are doing and can make a difference for your employees, and, consequently, for your organization.

4 Determine how often budgets for initiatives are cut after they are assigned, and then find out why this occurs. Ongoing budget cutting is a symptom of gaming the system, and employees see this and realize that this demonstrated behaviour is acceptable . . . which it should not be. Change your budget planning process to ensure that budget submissions are accurate and realistic, and then once the funds are targeted, keep the budgets intact. Anything else sends the signal to employees (and suppliers and customers) that management is incompetent to run an organization effectively over time.

5 Ensure that working collectively as teams is rewarded. Employees are not stupid, and if they believe that working collectively in teams is not rewarded, they won't do it. Clearly there will always be outstanding employees, but finding ways to reward teams is the only way to encourage collective team behaviours. Not advocating team behaviours will only create adversarial relationships, and the outcome of this can be extremely destructive to the organizational future.

6 Determine if initiatives that are begun are allowed to finish. When management is seen to pile new initiative upon new initiative, it can send the signal that they are not sure what they are doing, and that they would rather appear to be busy, scurrying around from this project to that project, than to do what they are paid to do. Sponsored (meaning management keeps coming up with new initiatives) non-completion of initiatives also sends the signal that management is grasping at straws, desperately looking for something that will improve organizational effectiveness. Too often, this 'flavour-of-the-day' initiative evolution is the principal reason that employees believe that management is not competent to manage. And when this occurs, motivation and commitment disappear, and stress increases rapidly.

The whole issue of managerial and employee workplace stress should not be minimized by senior management, and can be summed up with a simple reinforcing story: the greater the stress, the less able employees are to be effective, and the less effective they are, the greater the stress they will feel. The choice for management is easy. Either recognize that employee stress can be, and is, a serious problem that negatively impacts productivity and effectiveness (and then do something about it), or just keep getting the results they are getting. Only one of these answers makes the most sense to shareholders, Boards, suppliers and customers. The question is which of these answers make the most sense to management?

Questions

- Do managers and employees in your organization suffer from stress?
- What is the monetary cost of the stress in terms of lost time, mistakes being made, and lack of commitment to organization goals and management decisions?
- Is there an understanding of what is causing the stress?
- Is anything being done to reduce it?

Rushing to nowhere?

Avoiding the unintended consequences of change

Business trends are like riding the change pendulum – first you swing to one side, and then back to the other side. It would be nice to have the pendulum settle down, hopefully in the middle somewhere – a place called *rationality in business decision-making* – but it never seems to. It can be quite a blur, going back and forth. As a matter of fact, sometimes all this blurring of vision causes us to forget what has happened before.

If my memory serves me correctly, one of the really hot agenda items in business in the few past years has been to look at your company; and then take every process possible that isn't nailed down and outsource it. This has been a real boom for smaller organizations that specialize in certain services, like call centres, cheque processing, training, and you name it. The logic behind all this activity has been sound – if you can outsource some of your processes, you can save money and reduce some of the complexity of the business. Great thinking, but, as with many business decisions, the ones who rush into outsourcing at the speed of light tend to miss the bigger picture. And now, according to a recent study done by one of the big four (or is it five again?), '*70 per cent of participants had significant negative experiences with outsourcing. End users were disappointed with lack of cost savings, hidden costs and amount of management they had to supply to support the outsourcing project.*' Welcome to the land of reality.

Outsourcing *can* be a good thing. But there are more things to consider than just the obvious cost savings that might occur.

Business costs are basically a function of two factors: cost factor number 1 is associated with actually writing cheques. You know, when you actually *pay* for something. In many cases, cost factor number 1 can be reduced through outsourcing, actually, quite a bit from my experiences with senior management teams. Cost factor number 2 is not as obvious. This is where the costs are either disguised in the form of some other line item, or not even on a balance sheet. It is the last one that should be of most concern because most finance guys don't even apparently see them as legitimate costs. These costs include the cost attached to good (or bad) morale; good (or bad) long-term customer satisfaction; high (or low) ability to achieve alignment; and the most frightening, the high (or higher) costs that will be incurred to ensure that the outsourcing decision really can work.

Poor morale can occur due to the onset of the outsourcing bug; once it has started, employees in other departments begin to realize that they might be next, and they tend to lose their commitment to the business. They become disenchanted and their willingness to go the extra mile for internal or external customers falls apart quickly.

Customer satisfaction can wilt as soon as the customers discover that the people who they have been talking to regarding problems or requests are suddenly replaced by people who quite often have no clue what the issues are. I have seen this occur when I have tried to deal with outsourced airline reservations staff who have never been to, nor understand, some of the complexities of air travel in Europe. It is not a fun experience to have to deal with outsourced staff who know little about what they are talking about. Organizational alignment suffers because management is now dealing with multiple population groups in disparate locations (and in many cases, from disparate work ethic backgrounds).

Being able to impress upon an outsourced population the necessity for corporate alignment can be difficult, especially when the outsourcing company is working for more than one client. And the most potentially (financially) devastating impact is the hidden, unforeseen costs of trying to make sure the outsourcing decision works. Because few companies have a good grasp of the real costs associated with outsourcing, creep begins to set in. First it is the costs associated with correcting initial outsourcing problems, and then the problems continue to grow and the costs escalate.

As I said earlier, outsourcing *can be* a good decision, but only if the key decision-makers take into consideration what else might happen when the decision is made. Today I spent almost an hour in the post office in Knightsbridge in a monstrously long queue that had a sign that stated that 'due to cost reduction initiatives, two customer service clerks had been let go'. Fine. Reducing the number of people that take care of customers will save them money, but the resultant queues were as bad as the Christmas season. Customer service was the only topic of discussion in the queue. Would the Royal Mail's service improve if they were outsourced? Who knows, but it does seem to be under consideration. In a time when all organizations are focusing on how to reduce costs, outsourcing perhaps should be a consideration. But not because everyone else is doing it. Outsourcing should be considered if there is a cost crisis looming, but, the decision-makers need to be conscious of what else might happen if the outsourcing occurs. Reducing the potential for one serious crisis only to have another one arise may not be the smartest move.

Perhaps the ultimate test would be to have decision-makers who are considering outsourcing respond to what the real costs will be, and if they don't know, companies should outsource them.

Questions

- Does your organization currently outsource some services or production?
- What was the rationale for this decision?
- Have there been any unintended consequences of that decision?
- Are the unintended consequences good or bad for the organization in the long term?

Missing the signals?

Heading off crises before they land on your desk

Since the Boxing Day 2004 tsunami that wreaked devastation and killed countless thousands, quite a few initiatives are being considered to help ensure that this type of disaster could never happen again. Many of these ideas talk about an early warning system to alert local populaces of a disaster in the works. And yet, there were signals that were present – unfortunately, many of them were not recognized.

Shortly after the tsunami, I read of a remote village in Aceh where insects, birds and animals were all seen moving away from the seashore a full 30 minutes before the tidal wave hit. The villagers recognized this signal and disappeared into the jungle with the animals, without experiencing a single loss of life. This story can make one think of how often there are signals of impending organizational performance doom that *we don't recognize*.

In business, it is apparent that we are good at looking for key indicators of performance. But it is also apparent that in many cases, the indicators we look at do not give us enough warning to stop the financial haemorrhaging that can occur when performance sinks and then avoid the corresponding crisis. Clearly, we are looking at the wrong indicators.

'Seeing' indicators of looming problems is not that difficult. The trick is to think systemically about cause and effect relationships between the various indicators that are out there. Here is the way that this works. In business, a well-recognized indicator of impending doom is loss of market share. But what actually causes market share to fall? To find out, we need to begin to look backwards – loss of market share happens when customers go elsewhere for products or services. This, quite often, is due to competitive products or services being more attractive, but the question is, 'why?' One of the reasons is because your company may not have been able to deliver your new offering as fast as your competitors have. And this could be because your design or production team wasn't able to sort out the bugs in the new offering. Not being able to sort out new release problems usually stems from inadequate testing, which is a function of poor planning, i.e., not allowing for contingencies in the plan. This usually occurs because your 'planners' were under pressure to deliver, and rushed the process. And being under pressure is a direct function of an organizational culture that is under stress. So whilst the typically looked at indicator of 'loss of market share' might be worthwhile to keep your eyes open for, a sign that is equally visible, but visible far earlier, is the stress level of the organization.

The same or equally similar technique for determining early warning signals holds true for the typical service industry; not-for-profits; higher education; and all other sectors – regardless of size – look at the indicators you currently use to determine 'what might happen', and then go backwards until you find what really is driving potential problems.

Recently I met the CEO of a mid-sized organization who was very concerned because his organization was suffering from, he thought, wild, unforeseen fluctuations in energy prices. I suggested that we work through the process, and he balked at the idea. His reasoning was that they (his team) had been making sound progress in stabilizing his company until the price of crude oil began to escalate last year. 'This process may work fine for internally generated problems, but this is something that is way beyond our control', he responded. My view was different, and I walked him through it, using his 'problem' as the example. Only this time, there were only a few steps needed to discover where the problems really stemmed from.

Profits falling due to increasing costs, due to escalating oil prices, stemming from the lack of planning on his team's part that this *could actually occur*. His team, because they had been doing so well in building their business, had become lulled into thinking that they could do no wrong; that they were infallible, and nothing could stop the meteoric profit rise. The early warning signal was that their growth plans *didn't contain any contingency planning*.

In most cases, the true indicators worth watching for all point to organizational culture and the lack of leadership. But because it is easier to just look for indicators that are less 'threatening' to management's ability to manage, we tend to look for the more obvious ones. Quite a pity, because so many of the problems experienced by business can be avoided . . . if we are just willing to see the *real* underlying signals.

Questions

- What indicators do your decision-makers use to know where the organization is?
- Are the indicators ones that represent high or low leverage elements of the business?
- How do you know?
- What indicators of potential problems that may inhibit the organization's ability to satisfy its mission are available but not being observed? Why not?
- How difficult would it be to change the choice of key indicators?

Skilled incompetence: is it still alive?

Getting things right, the first time

In a recent study by Collinson Grant published in *Personnel Today*, it was disclosed that the Foreign Office is apparently taking a cue from business: '*(The FO is) an organization slow to act, suffering from a lack of delegation and few professional managers. The leaders focus primarily on their diplomatic and political duties, rarely on the efficient management of the organization.*'

'*People are frustrated and impeded in the execution of critical tasks by the weakness of the organization, yet are unwilling to tackle the root causes that are entrenched in, and reinforced by, the established culture. The entire organization needs to be challenged and reformed but the leadership lacks the skills needed and the will to upset the status quo.*' So reassuring for us taxpayers.

I could go on for pages about how nice it is that government is actually learning about performance from business, but this study does show that some of what is being learned is not good. And even worse is the knowledge that these behaviours are still rampant in business organizations . . . which they are. The problem lies in which business behaviours are not good.

Too often, business managers are mired in reactive thinking, firefighting, and trying to hold on to the status quo instead of working collectively to achieve strategic goals and initiatives that are critical if an organization is going to do what it is supposed to be doing for customers, shareholders, and to sustain good supplier relationships. Instead of helping the organization realize its potential, managers who exhibit these behaviours are wasting time and resources – both of which few organizations can afford to lose today. These misdirected efforts can only be termed *skilled incompetence*.

The whole issue around what is known as skilled incompetence runs through organizations from all sectors, of all sizes, and is probably just as prevalent in the east as it is in the west. The term 'skilled incompetence' was coined by Chris Argyris in the early 1990s as a way to explain managerial behaviours, whereby managers use practised routine behaviour (skill) to produce what they do not intend (incompetence). In practice, this materializes in such examples as managers who do not plan for future scenarios that might negatively impact their organization; managers who still believe good communication means telling employees that they need to work harder; managers who would rather fight over scarce resources than try to figure out how to share them in the most effective way; and managers that never seem to deliver because they would rather sit in their offices than to get out to the front-lines where the real work is being done. The outcomes of these examples (all taken from recent reports in the media about company results) are less-than-committed employees and poor organizational performance.

Skilled incompetence rears it ugly head when managers lose the plot about what is important, and why. I have met with many managers from organizations of all types who seem to believe that their first responsibility is to protect their own turf. When this occurs, resources, whether human resources (knowledge, wisdom, and just plain warm bodies) and financial resources (fixed budgets, investments, and miscellaneous discretionary spend items) become just pawns in the game of 'who wins'.

In order to eliminate the belief that management is all about turf, managers first need to understand that the *only* way they win is if the entire organization wins. Resources are dedicated to managers for the express purpose of *helping the entire organization achieve its goals*; not so that one manager or another can build his or her own fiefdom of organizational power and control. Managers need to learn that they not only need to achieve their own goals and targets, but they also need to ensure that in that process, they do not demonstrate actions or behaviours that will result in other managers not being able to achieve goals and targets. Managers who don't, for some reason, understand this point, need to be given the opportunity to change their behaviours; and if they don't, they need to be sent away. Organizations today simply cannot afford to have managers who do not believe that they are just part of a greater whole, and their principle job is to ensure that what they do supports the overall organizational direction.

In all fairness, senior management needs to recognize that ensuring that its teams demonstrate appropriate behaviour is a function of demonstrating it themselves. Ensuring that actions are taken that are congruent with organizational goals; ensuring that decisions are checked for negative unintended consequences *before* they are implemented; ensuring that managers have adequate resources to achieve what they are asked to achieve; and treating managers with appropriate respect are all signals that employees see and respond to. And if employees don't see these signals, it is not surprising that they assume that 'do as I say and not as I do' is the operating philosophy of the organization, and then they will respond in kind.

Next, managers need to change the way they think about issues and challenges; change the way they influence employees and suppliers about what is truly important to the organization; change the way they achieve goals and targets that are crucial for overall organizational success; and change the way they demonstrate leadership. Employees follow managerial directions because they are willing to be compliant. However, employees follow leaders because they understand why the strategic direction of the organization is important, and they see how they fit into that picture. At the end of the day, the organizations that are able to be sustainable – to achieve positive gains, and *keep those gains over time* – will be run by people who understand the dynamics of change; who are able to create environments in which crises do not occur; and environments in which the organization and its people can realize their individual and collective potential.

155
being competent to
survive it all
08

Questions

- Does your management team deliver on the promise of sustainable high results?
- Have they created an environment in which the organization can realize its potential?
- Do you believe they are the best people to run the business?

Have you tied your own hands?

Inhibiting our own ability to deal with change and avoid crises

Just as I was finishing this book, I heard from a manager at a medium-sized marketing company with a problem. He had recently taken a position as communications director for a large European company, and he related to me one of the challenges that many companies face, a challenge that has been festering for several years, and the lack of resolution to it was fast approaching crisis status.

His remit was quite specific – to develop a sound internal communications methodology. The company had been showing incredible growth and its senior managers recognized the need to improve internal communications. And whilst he did identify and map out a successful way forward, he also encountered some serious unintended consequences of the solution.

The plan was to figure out a way to get the message out about the company's strategic direction, but it didn't take long for him to see that the infrastructure to do this didn't support the goal. There were inconsistencies from department to department; some managers had a solid sense of the strategy and did share that view; but whilst others had a view, they had been less-than-effective in sharing it; and some departmental managers didn't even see the entire strategic picture. It was clear why a crisis was looming.

The challenge my friend faced was complicated by the very success of the company. As the company had grown, quite naturally, the workload for many managers and employees increased, and this increase in workload had begun to sap morale and, over time, employee retention had become an issue. An increasing turnover in employee and managerial ranks meant keeping the strategic message clear had become even more problematic. So senior management ensured that budget managers were given funds targeted to improving communications and learning, but the growth of the business meant that time to communicate and learn was surpassed by the need to keep the growth engine accelerating. My friend's path of choice was to engage managers and employees.

Engaging a workforce can be challenging itself, but the rewards from doing this can pay huge dividends. Initially, the challenge is to find out exactly who knows what in the organization. This can be done through surveys, but the end product too often resembles what employees think that managers want to see. A more effective way to determine the real depth of knowledge about where a company is going, why it is going in that direction, and how it will get there, is to hold small meeting conversations.

Assemble small cross-sectional groups of the organizational population, and ask them how the company functions. This will yield a series of organizational 'variables' – elements of the business that can either improve or decline over time. By linking them together with arrows, it is possible to illuminate how that group of people see the business operating. And by doing this with multiple cross-sectional groups, it is relatively easy to gain an understanding of the similarities or variances in workforce understanding of where the company is, and where it is going. An additional benefit of these conversations is that the people in each individual group begin to 'see' other managerial and employee views on the situation. This type of learning, *peer-to-peer learning*, is far more effective than simply trying to 'tell' people what you want them to know.

Once you have an understanding of the collective view of the organizational situation, you can then plan specific events targeted to expand that understanding across the business.

In situation, the director had put together a combination of events: specific strategy days – meetings targeted on deploying a common vision of the organizational strategy; and 'company away days' – meetings targeted to combining shared learning and build additional alignment on where the company was going, and how it would get there.

One of the keys to ensuring that a company can realize its potential is to ensure that managers and employees alike have a shared understanding of what the organizational strategy is. And the first step to do this is to determine what and how much they know about it.

Unfortunately, if you don't engage the workforce, this can be brutally difficult to do. But by letting them share their views of how the business really works, and then building a programme around that baseline, it is possible to not only engage the workforce in the process, but to engage them in a way that they accept the strategic challenge and make it theirs. This makes far more sense than letting an existing communications infrastructure keep your hands tied.

Questions

- Is your workforce fully engaged in strategic and tactical initiatives?
- Are they engaged in the organization's communications process?
- If not, what are some of the roadblocks to engaging them?
- How could you get past those roadblocks?
- What else might occur when you try to close the 'engagement gap'?

part 4

structures and
worksheets

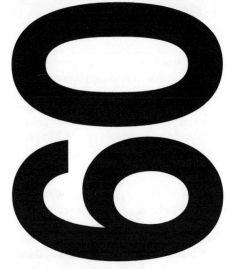

09
structures that impact performance

In this chapter you will learn:

- what is behind structure-
  driving behaviour
- how to use structural
  understandings to ensure
  better outcomes
- which structures provide the
  strongest leverage

The downside of stepping in

The story

In many companies, the process used to deploy initiatives is to delegate the tasks to teams. On the surface, the process is quite clear: explain to the team what needs to be done, give them the resources needed, and wait for the results. However, quite often, the planned initiative deployment process fails. Often, when this occurs, a manager will step in to drive the deployment himself.

The outcomes

Whilst this may ensure that the initiative is put forth, two of the unintended consequences are that the team will never acquire the experience needed to do this effectively in the future, and the manager will never give them the opportunity to learn. Additionally, there can be the expectation that the manager will intervene again in the future, negating the willingness of the team members to put forth appropriate effort, whilst at the same time, setting the manager up for failure due to over extending himself. All unintended consequences can create fundamentally systemic long-term problems relating to the growth potential of the organization, and short-term problems in the willingness of employees to be committed to organizational goals.

The structure driving these performance behaviours is shown in Figure 18.

Solutions

Prior to the deployment process:

- Ensure that teams charged with initiatives have an appropriate level of skills and resources to get the job done on time, in full.
- Ensure that the team members have a full understanding of what needs to be done, by when, what the measures of success will be, and why the initiative is important; i.e., how the initiative connects to the vision of the organization.
- Ensure that potential roadblocks to success are removed before they are encountered.

After the deployment process:

- Hold a debrief review of how the deployment process went, both for the team and the managers involved in the process.

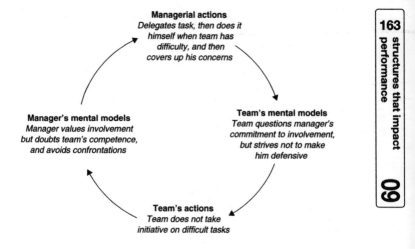

Managerial actions
Delegates task, then does it himself when team has difficulty, and then covers up his concerns

Manager's mental models
Manager values involvement but doubts team's competence, and avoids confrontations

Team's mental models
Team questions manager's commitment to involvement, but strives not to make him defensive

Team's actions
Team does not take initiative on difficult tasks

Figure 18

- Find out what lessons have been learned that can be shared with other parts of the organization. Share them.
- Look for any unintended consequences from the deployment process.

Long-term positioning:

- Train managers and employees in ways to identify potential implementation problems before they are encountered.
- Train managers and employees in ways to understand the impact of mental models on performance, motivation, alignment and commitment.
- Train managers and employees in communication skills, most notably, empathic listening, asking non-threatening questions, left-hand column, and ladder of inference.
- Create time and space for teams to 'practise' implementing initiatives. By enabling teams to simulate the deployment process, they gain valuable experience and increase both their experience and confidence.

The problems with the 'quick-fix'

The story

Sales were down; and because of it, revenues, and consequently, profits were slipping. Management put pressure on the sales

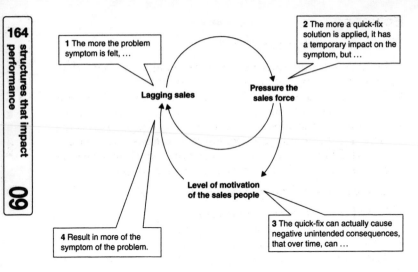

Figure 19

force to achieve the numbers that had been put forth as sales goals. And yet, the sales dropped even further, and because of it, more pressure was applied, this time with the sales force being measured on how many client meetings they set each week. The new metric appeared to be hit, but sales didn't improve.

The issue

By focusing on 'quick-fix' solutions to ongoing problems, too often the action that is taken to resolve the problem only aggravates the situation. This is because many managers attack the symptom of the problem, and not the problem itself. In this case, the problem symptom was lagging sales, but the solution that management applied only made the problem worse.

The more management felt the pressure of lagging sales, the more they put pressure on the sales people. Whilst this sometimes would result in sales 'spikes' (the short-term fix), over time, the sales people lost their motivation and just went through the actions of having meetings, but not closing the deals.

The structure driving these performance behaviours is shown in Figure 19.

Solutions

Prior to the problem occurring:

- Ensure that your sales people understand how their efforts contribute to overall organizational success.
- Ensure that your sales people have a complete knowledge of your product lines, and how they can help address customers' needs.
- Use sales performance metrics that encourage both actual sales and the building of long-term relationships with customers. Long-term relationships pay off, especially when customers are given relatively equal choices in suppliers.

After the problem has been recognized:

- Look for the problem, but then check to ensure that what you see is not just the symptom of the problem.
- Identify systemic solutions to fundamental problems.
- Test the solutions before implementing them to avoid unintended consequences (such as seen in the story).

Long-term positioning to avoid the problem:

- Train your sales people in listening skills.
- Equip your sales people with the ability to understand not only the words the customers say, but what is behind those words. The ability to listen empathically is a key sales tool.
- Focus your sales people on creating an environment in which your customers can buy from you, instead of trying to sell them something. Sales efforts are quite often easier to resist than environments in which customers see the need, and make the connection to your ability to meet that need.
- Encourage your sales people to think of customers as partners in long-term, win–win business arrangements instead of just vehicles to meet sales targets.
- Train management in systemic thinking so that they can avoid repeat problems over time.

Dealing with the hiring conundrum

The story

Mr Smith's company was growing, and at the same time, he had a problem with employee retention. Additional employees would be hired, but a substantial percentage of them left within six months, causing him to hire more people. And because he was so

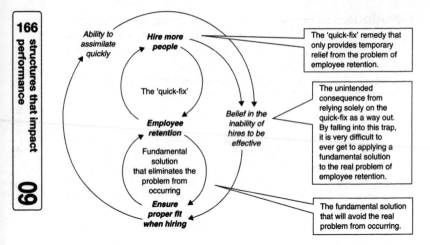

The 'quick-fix' remedy that only provides temporary relief from the problem of employee retention.

The unintended consequence from relying solely on the quick-fix as a way out. By falling into this trap, it is very difficult to ever get to applying a fundamental solution to the real problem of employee retention.

The fundamental solution that will avoid the real problem from occurring.

Figure 20

occupied trying to keep growing the company, he ended up having a standing order with an employment agency.

The issue

Making sure that the people you hire will actually stay on the job is just a symptom of a deeper issue – how to ensure that the people you hire will provide the right fit for your company. If you don't take the time to determine if your hires can and will connect with where your company is going, it is easy to fall into the trap of believing that new hires are not competent, and consequently, keep hiring more people. This becomes a vicious cycle which wastes time, money, people resources, and damages the chances of having a stable, productive workforce.

The structure driving these performance behaviours is shown in Figure 20.

Solutions

Prior to the problem occurring:

- When looking for new hires, find out if they have both the appropriate technical skills to do the job, but also if they clearly understand where the company is going, and why it is going there.

- Ensure that whomever in your organization conducts hiring interviews has the ability to ask both closed questions ('do you know how to . . .?') and open questions ('how could your efforts help the company to . . .?').
- Find out how easy (or difficult) it is for a new hire to assimilate into your organizational culture.

After the problem has been recognized:

- Do 'leaving' interviews to see why the employee chose to leave, or, if the employee was sacked, find out what obstacles he or she encountered that blocked his or her ability to perform.
- Take a look at the criteria you have been using for screening new hires. Check to see if these criteria are appropriate for the position(s) you are trying to fill.
- Understand what performance structure is causing the problem to occur.

Long-term positioning to avoid the problem:

- Determine what skills are really needed from new hires. This list should include both the specific technical skills needed to do the job, but also skills in the area of communications, listening and thinking.
- Ensure that all new hires – before they begin work – are provided with a clear picture of where the company is going, why that is important, how it will get there, and how their contributions will support that desired future.
- Use some form of peer support to help new hires assimilate into your company culture.
- Work with your managers to help them acquire solid skills in the area of thinking and influencing.
- Build a team-based culture where team contributions are valued over 'hero' or individual success thinking.

Changing mental models

The story

After several turbulent years of demonstrating very directive management, the CEO decided that he wanted to work on improving the culture of the organization. But no matter what he tried, the employees didn't believe that his 'new style' of managing was sincere. The organizational climate kept sinking, due to the expectation that soon he would resort to being a dictator.

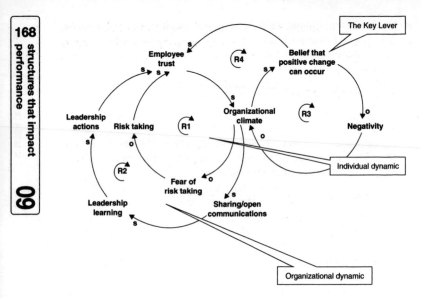

Figure 21

The issue

Changing an organizational culture takes time, and requires clear demonstrable leadership behaviours. When a culture improves, more open sharing of important communications takes place, ensuring that senior people can learn more of what needs to be done to improve further. Over time, this builds trust, and eventually, can help managers and employees actually believe that the culture has improved, thus allowing it to improve further. The key is creating an environment in which people *can believe* that positive change can occur. If they do not believe that senior people can change their behaviours, they will see no reason to change their own behaviours, with the end result being that performance suffers.

The structure driving these performance behaviours is shown in Figure 21.

Solutions

Prior to the problem occurring:

• Identify what types of behaviours should be expected from employees and managers alike. This includes the most senior managers.

- Find a way to measure the current and sought-after behaviours.
- Set up a process with which to help employees and managers to change their behaviours if they are out of sync with what is needed.

After the problem has been recognized:

- When employees or managers are found to be demonstrating behaviours that are counter-productive, or not in alignment with company values, have someone internally coach them. If you do not have anyone internal that has the right skills to coach, bring in an outside coach.

Long-term positioning to avoid the problem:

- Openly discuss desired behaviours in meetings. If the subject is avoided, behaviours will become an organizational 'undiscussable' that, over time, can have serious long-term impacts on alignment and commitment to goals and initiatives.
- In meetings, discuss how mental models are formed, and re-formed. Work with tools such as Ladder-of-Inference and Left-Hand Column to explain how mental models are arrived at, and how to use them to help change existing mental models to ones that are more congruent with and supportive of organizational values.

Pressure: the risk of backfiring

The story

The company had being seeing its performance sink, and soon senior management was told to put some pressure on to deliver results. But the more pressure that management put on the employees to improve, the more the performance sank. And as with most cases of quick-fixes not working, management then upped the pressure more, assuming that this would do the trick, and yet performance continued to be erratic.

The issue

Using pressure to improve performance can work, but it rarely works over time. The more we put pressure on people to do something, the more they fear even further pressure if things don't go right; and because of this, they develop a 'bunker mentality', doing only what they have to do to get by. The bunker

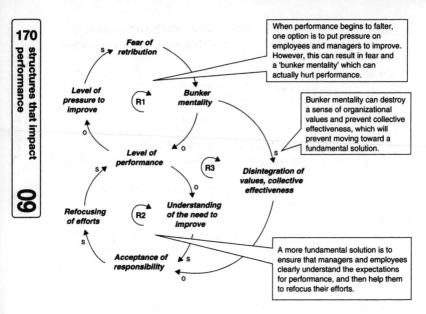

Figure 22

mentality not only diverts efforts from high performance, but it can also disintegrate company values and collective effectiveness. They only sound path forward is to create an environment in which employees accept responsibility for individual and collective performance.

The structure driving these performance behaviours is shown in Figure 22.

Solutions

Prior to the problem occurring:

- Ensure that all managers and employees have a clear understanding of the performance expectations of the organization.
- Determine appropriate method to measure performance.
- Conduct informal checks of organizational culture (coffee-machine conversations).

After the problem has been recognized:

- Before pressure is applied to improve performance, find out why it isn't being delivered. It could be a lack of skills, a lack

of resources, a lack of understanding, excessive variation in organizational processes and/or systems, or internal conflicts that are counter-productive.
- Engage employees in finding solutions – this will demonstrate leadership on your part, and result in a better solution that can avoid the problem resurfacing in the future.

Long-term positioning to avoid the problem:

- When developing strategic and tactical goals, identify what levels of performance will be needed to achieve the sought-after performance.
- Have a baseline for organizational culture, including motivation and commitment to organizational goals.
- Implement semi-annual surveys to measure culture.
- Talk about the potential for bunker mentality and defence mechanisms at team meetings, as well as how to avoid them from occurring.

Prioritizing investment decisions: training

The story

The company was faced with figuring out where to cut costs to save money, and in the first decision meeting, one of the managers suggested that they cut out training. 'We can resume it as soon as profitability returns', he said. But another manager said that in his previous company, when training was cut, it was never started again, and he thought that one of the reasons that his old company went out of business was that their competition had lower production costs, due largely to a well-trained workforce. And yet, most of the managers said that training should go, even if temporarily.

The issue

All companies make investments: capital equipment, buildings and building customer relationships. And whilst all these are important, unless the company has a skilled workforce, it will never be able to be competitive over time. Note: 'skilled' means that they have learnt the best way to be effective in using the organizational processes and systems, *and* know how to communicate effectively, how they fit into (and support) the organizational vision, and understand the ramifications of their actions.

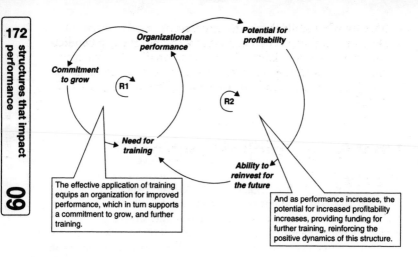

Figure 23

The structure driving these performance behaviours is shown in Figure 23.

Solutions

Prior to the problem occurring:

- Ensure that all employees and managers have the ability to participate in structured training, whether offered internally as part of a company programme, or externally through contractors or educational institutions.
- Ensure that all employees and managers have a structured personal and organizationally-focused growth plan.
- Demonstrate a commitment to training by participating yourself.

After the problem has been recognized:

- If a training programme has been cut in order to reduce costs, reinstate it as soon as possible. However, it is important to recognize that any gap in training can give competition a clear advantage, so the best option is to not cut it at all.

Long-term positioning to avoid the problem:

- Determine what skills managers and employees will need if the company is going to be able to realize its potential.

- Identify what skills they currently have.
- Develop a training programme that will close the gap between current and needed skills. Whilst 'operational' skills are important and should not be neglected, ensure that communications, thinking, influencing, listening, and coaching skills are included.

Identifying structural tension

The story

Faced with conflicting options for how to make better decisions, the relatively new CEO was torn between keeping a tight rein on spending appropriations and delegating this responsibility to his local site managers. This issue had been growing ever since the company had come out of a near bankruptcy situation in which the CEO had taken control of everything in order to rebuild the company, which had included sacking quite a few decision-makers who had contributed to the mess the company had found itself in. The local managers who had survived believed that they had demonstrated fiscal responsibility through the 'survival period' and were now keen to regain the control over local decisions that they were being held responsible for. And yet, the CEO was still concerned that letting go of all the control too soon might let the company slip once again – something he was not prepared to let happen.

The issue

The CEO was faced with the dynamic of structural tension. There were sound reasons for him to continue to have control, and yet there were equally sound reasons for him to delegate the local control to local managers. Structural tension manifests itself in situations where one vein of rational thinking dictates one path, whilst at the same time, another opposite vein of equally rational thinking dictates an opposing path.

The decision was complicated by the fact that the organization's finance people were of the belief that decisions around spend should remain in the realm of control of the head office, and this belief had, over time, built in delays into the requisition approval process.

The structure driving these performance behaviours

The dilemma facing the CEO was to determine which decision path to take, and equally, help the centralized and local finance people, as well as local managers, understand the rationale for his decision. The structural model (Figure 24) shows that each path does make sense: if one of the goals is to rebuild the organization through growing the company, it makes sense to put the decision authority in the hands of local managers who should have a better feel of what investments are needed to sustain the growth. However, if one of the goals is to guard precious financial resources, it also makes clear sense to have the central decision authority retain control over spending. The tension dilemma occurs in the fact that both goals are valid and in the case of most organizations, extremely important – companies need to grow, and they need to guard their finances whilst doing so. It is the decisions that accompany each goal that drive the tension. If you delegate financial decision-making, it is more difficult to ensure that resources are being applied in a way that can support the overall organization; and if you keep control over the spending, it is difficult to ensure that local needs are being met. It is the classic dilemma of trying to figure out how to have your cake and eat it too.

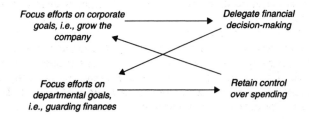

Figure 24

Solutions

Prior to the problem occurring:

- Ensure that all decision-makers are in alignment with why specific decisions have been made, and if they are limited in time, ensure that they understand what that time limit will be.
- Do not delay, unless for sound reason, the resumption of previous decision-making authority. If the resumption needs to be

delayed for specific reason(s), communicate that reason clearly to all decision-makers who will be impacted by it.

- Ensure that managers are able to demonstrate their competence to deliver the performance they will be measured on.

After the problem has been recognized:

- In order to avoid the sense that key decisions are being delayed or withheld, hold sessions with decision-makers to explain what the structural tension elements are, and why they are occurring. Ask for their input as to ways that the tension can be resolved. Build alignment around the tension resolution decision.
- Use the structural tension model to help improve understanding. This may require the development of several different versions of the same tension, but if they are developed by the decision-makers in the sessions, the ability to build consensus and support for the decision outcome will be increased.

Long-term positioning to avoid the problem:

- Ensure that all managers impacted by cross-organizational issues (finance decision-makers, whether local or centralized and local and centralized finance people in this example), have a common understanding of their explicit and implicit roles in the company. In the example, one of the aggravating factors to the problem of where to put the finance decision-making authority was that the finance people in the subject company had adopted their implicit roles as their focus. Their explicit roles were to ensure that finances were managed to ensure that the company would be able to achieve its missions, but their implicit roles had become the 'guardians' of funding, and because of this, were slowing down the CEO's already-in-place sign off on requests policy.

The possible confusion of explicit and implicit organizational roles can diminish the ability of an organization to realize its potential, regardless of where in the organization managers function.

10

worksheets

In this chapter you will learn:

- how to take the ambiguity out of decision-making
- how to facilitate effective decision-making
- how to use worksheets to ensure better outcomes

Left-hand column

Often when senior managers or business leaders speak to managers and employees, there is a disconnection between what is said, and what is understood. The downside of this can be misdirected efforts to implement a strategy or initiative; damage to motivation, alignment and organizational culture; and inappropriate mental models being formulated about senior managerial intent or competence.

In order to help alleviate this problem, a tool can be used to 'test' if there is a gap between what is said, and what is 'heard' or understood. The tool is known as 'left-hand column'. Left-hand column, developed by Chris Argyris in the late 1980s, can be used in small team meetings, as well as large, organizational-wide meetings. Additionally, the left-hand column can be used to test understanding in written communications.

The basis for left-hand column comes from the belief that when we hear or read some information, we make assumptions on what is behind the information, or on how we interpret what is being communicated. To use the left-hand column tool for meetings, it is important to know what the speaker will be saying prior to the talk.

The key elements of the verbal or written communications are selected and placed in the right-hand column of a sheet of A4 paper. The left-hand column of the paper is left open. The A4s are then distributed to a group of recipients of the written communications, or a group of people who are present at a meeting or speech. Participants are then asked to write (in the left-hand column of the sheet) how they are interpreting the message(s).

Things to watch for when using the left-hand column tool:

- Only select key elements of the communications. Key elements might include expectations of the person making the communications, reasons and rationale for strategic direction or implementation goals, and updates on current company situations.
- Select a cross-sectional group of people to fill out the left-hand column tool. The reason for this is to ensure that what is observed is accurate.
- Do not use the left-hand column tool as a way to determine who in your organization 'is not onboard' with communications. The purpose is to understand how recipients of communications actually interpret what is being said, whether verbally or in writing.

What I interpret this to mean	What was communicated
We know that competition is getting harder to deal with, but why wasn't someone watching them? Isn't that part of the boss's job to know what is happening?	'We know that competition is getting harder, the competition out there is eating us alive and we have to do something . . .'
If we keep changing our strategy, how will we ever manage to keep our people focused on doing the right things?	'We are going to revise our strategy so we can gain more market share . . .'
We are all working extra time right now. How much more effort can we put in before we decide that it isn't worth it. If you would give us the resources we need, we could be more effective.	It is time for all of us to put in extra effort so we can survive . . .'
Why is it that the only people whose goals are going to increase are the people in the production area? Why can't the guys in the office have their performance improve too?	'We are going to increase performance goals by 10 per cent for all production staff . . .'
A nice offer, but the last time I asked for funds to train my people, I was told that we don't have any more money to spend on training. That is what we need to do – train our people so we can keep up with the competition.	'Tell me what I can do to help you become more effective . . .'

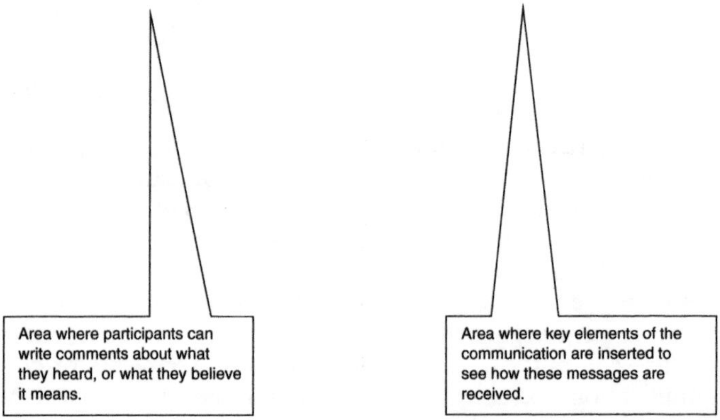

Area where participants can write comments about what they heard, or what they believe it means.

Area where key elements of the communication are inserted to see how these messages are received.

Figure 25

What I interpret this to mean	What was communicated

Figure 26

- Ensure that participants who fill out the left-hand column tool do so with the utmost confidentiality. No names, no identifiers of any kind – only an honest reporting of how communications are understood.

As can be seen in this sample of the left-hand column tool, whilst the messages in the right-hand column appear to be quite clear, what is being 'heard' is a symptom of an organization in which managers and employees believe that senior management is either out of touch with what is going on, or is not doing what they should be doing. Either assumption can lead to a workforce that is not committed to organizational goals, and, therefore, will not be able to contribute effectively to organizational sustainability.

Figure 25 is an example of a completed left-hand column, and Figure 26 is a blank version. As stated in the Preface, full size copies of the worksheet templates can be found at www.rieley.com, Resources link.

An alignment matrix

Establishing a baseline for organizational alignment is important, especially when the organization is undergoing ongoing change efforts (which they actually all are). Too often, the understanding of alignment behind change issues is not clear and, consequently, it can be difficult to shift organizational behaviours. And equally often, there is little or no effort invested in finding out 'where' management and staff are regarding commitment to change.

A method that can be used to determine the level of commitment to change acceptance and commitment can be facilitated in several hours. The process involves sheets of A4 paper with a simple 2 × 2 grid matrix printed on it, and short conversations with a cross-section of management and employees.

Each participant in this process is given a copy of the matrix paper and asked to indicate where he or she believes the members of the senior management team are (or any other population group in the organization).

After a cross-section of people have filled out the matrix, the papers are collected and the responses are 'averaged out', and the resultant information is plotted on a master sheet. Now, in all fairness, there are some people who would take issue with this process. Their concerns are typically: (a) the process is very subjective; and (b) by identifying what the mental models are of others, some people may become defensive. Fair concerns, but when the subject of research is the mental models of employees – a subjective area to begin with – the perceptions of others are completely valid. We take actions based on what we perceive as much as we do on data, so it stands to reason that if we *believe* that some people are not committed to an initiative, we will act accordingly and probably not put forth additional effort with them.

The second concern is equally without merit, as no identification is asked for. Participants are only asked to put an identifying symbol someplace on the matrix to represent the perceived level of commitment of the members of the subject group.

A completed matrix can look like the example shown in Figure 27. In this example, the black circles represent where various members of the senior management team 'are' regarding their ability and willingness to be committed to a change effort. The open circles represent the members of a group of managers and

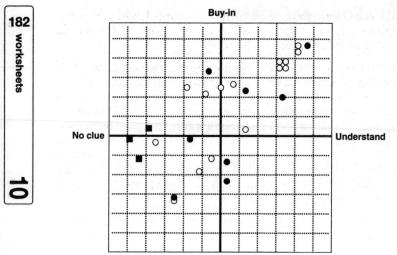

Figure 27

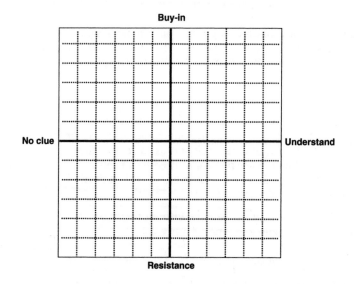

Figure 28

employees who were team members charged with an actual implementation project, and the black squares represent the union leadership in the organization.

After the composite matrix was put together, a meeting was held in which all the members of the senior team, the change team, and the union leadership were brought together . . . and the matrix was revealed. Initial comments included defensive responses about why some dots were where they were on the part of some team members, as well as denial statement about what the matrix displayed. But after a few minutes, it was clear to everyone that regardless of the actual accuracy of the dot locations on the matrix, the company was not well postured to ensure that the change effort would work.

Figure 28 is an uncompleted version of the matrix. The full size template can be found at www.rieley.com, Resources link.

Knowing when to let go

Many of us tend to believe that we can do it all. Well, at least we would like to think we can do it all. Surprise, surprise . . . we can't. I used to think I could, but one day I noticed that whilst I was doing more, what I thought I was doing wasn't getting done. Or at very minimum, it wasn't getting done well. And yet, being a semi-over-achiever, I didn't want to let anything go. After all, most people who think they can do it all also believe that no one else can do it as well. But as my personal performance sank little by little, I finally came to the realization that if my company was to continue to succeed, I would have to delegate more to others.

Delegation is a good thing, but it can be a painful process. I first made a list of all the things I was involved in, and then decided that I would delegate things that I wasn't able to do as well as I should. But after looking at the list, I realized that some of those things were activities that I really liked to do. I then sat down with a few of my managers and asked them which of my activities they thought they would be willing to pick up. A good group of people, and each of them said that they would be willing to take over one of the tasks I was doing. A nice thought, but I soon realized that the activities they were selecting weren't necessarily ones that I thought they would do as well as I had been doing. Clearly, if I was to be able to delegate at all, I would have to have a better process.

The next day, I met with the same managers again, and this time, asked them which activities that I was performing they thought I was doing well. As a CEO, this can be a touchy question, as many managers might feel the correct answer was, 'all of them boss'. To avoid this, I had made up a list of my activities and photocopied it for each of them. All they had to do was tick off the boxes that reflected the activities that *they* felt I did well. There was no pressure, no risk on their part, and no way I would have to deal with the sound of a great sucking in of breath coming from their mouths. I said thank you to all of them and took the check-sheets home with me. That night, I matched up what they had said with my list of activities I really liked to do, and then matched that up with the activities I spent the most amount of time on. Suddenly it became clear which activities to delegate to others.

It made sense for me to perform activities I liked to do, but only if I was competent in doing them. And it also made sense to double-check this against how much available time I really had.

It didn't take too long for my performance to get back to where I wanted it to be (and my company needed it to be).

The worksheet shown in Figure 29 has columns for:

1 the activities you perform during an average week;
2 ranked activities in which you have high levels of competence (do not make these judgements yourself – get outside input on what they are);
3 ranked activities you spend the most amount of time on;
4 ranked activities you like to do the most; and
5 activities you will delegate away.

You need to be honest and reasonable in your rankings for numbers 3 and 4, and then use the data to make sound decisions.

The full size template of the worksheet shown in Figure 29 can be found at www.rieley.com, Resources link.

Listing of activities you perform in an average week	Activities in which you have high competence	Activities you spend the most amount of time on	Activities you like to do the most	Delegate away

Figure 29

Ladder of inference

When organizations are working through any kind of change initiative (and in this case, change can include changing the way managers and employees do what they do), one of the problems that they encounter is trying to understand why some managers and/or employees react the way in which they do. Being able to understand is the first step in making the change process work.

It has often been said that 'people jump to conclusions', and in some regard, this statement is true. However, it is believed that whilst this occurs very quickly, it follows a very defined process. This process is akin to moving up a ladder (see Figure 30).

We begin the process with observable data – what we hear, see, or read is all considered to be observable data. We then select certain parts of the data to focus on. This focusing is not done with specific thought, but instead just occurs based on what we believe is worth considering. From the data we select, we begin to add meanings to what we see, hear or read. From these meanings, we begin to make assumptions, draw conclusions and adopt beliefs. We then do something. And because all of this takes place in our minds, the process takes less time that it does to snap your

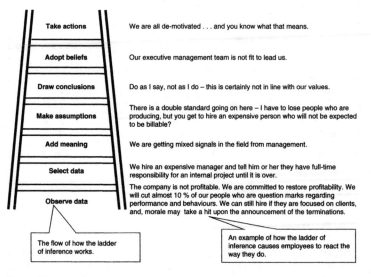

Take actions	We are all de-motivated . . . and you know what that means.
Adopt beliefs	Our executive management team is not fit to lead us.
Draw conclusions	Do as I say, not as I do – this is certainly not in line with our values.
Make assumptions	There is a double standard going on here – I have to lose people who are producing, but you get to hire an expensive person who will not be expected to be billable?
Add meaning	We are getting mixed signals in the field from management.
Select data	We hire an expensive manager and tell him or her they have full-time responsibility for an internal project until it is over.
Observe data	The company is not profitable. We are committed to restore profitability. We will cut almost 10 % of our people who are question marks regarding performance and behaviours. We can still hire if they are focused on clients, and, morale may take a hit upon the announcement of the terminations.

The flow of how the ladder of inference works.

An example of how the ladder of inference causes employees to react the way they do.

Figure 30

Instructions: Participant must write appropriate observations for each 'rung' of the ladder based on a specific event that resulted in an action being taken.

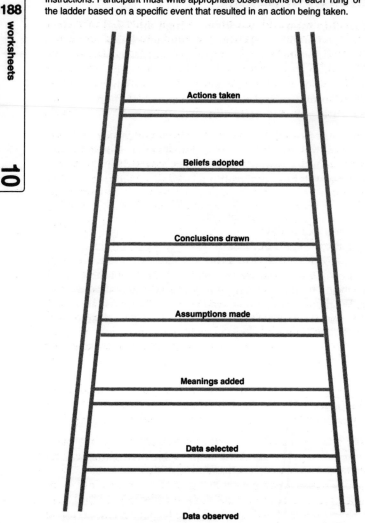

Actions taken

Beliefs adopted

Conclusions drawn

Assumptions made

Meanings added

Data selected

Data observed

Figure 31　Ladder of inference

fingers. What is fascinating, is that the beliefs we adopt have a very powerful influence on what data we select, and cause us to reinforce specific beliefs. (The full size template of the ladder of inference shown in Figure 31 can be found at www.rieley.com, Resources link.)

What are we doing?

In today's business world, one of the explicit skills that managers and employees 'need' to have is the ability to solve problems. Actually, that might be an understatement; what many organizations look for and reward, is the ability to be a proficient fire-fighter. Not fires in the literal sense, but organizational fires. Fire-fighting, or more importantly solving problems, has become a mark of high skill and something that employers want to see.

Ironically, fire-fighting is something that can be highly counter-productive, largely because many of the fires that managers and employees fight are the same ones that either they or someone else has fought before. And unless my mental definition powers are failing me, these highly-regarded people aren't solving problems at all – they are simply spending valuable time making organizational fires appear to go away, only to reappear at a later time; usually when the fire-fighter has moved on to tackle some other urgent problem. This process is, as we say, pure folly.

When faced with a serious organizational problem, one has a choice: either to completely resolve it so that it does not surface once again, or just address the symptoms of the problem with a quick-fix resolution and move on, hoping that the problem will take care of itself. This is like deciding to put an actual fire out, but leaving a litre of petrol next to the burning embers. The excuse for quick-fix fire-fighting is usually that managers and employees either don't have the skills to fully understand the root cause of the problem, or they are faced with so many fires that they need to 'do what they can and move on to the next one'. Either excuse – and that is what they both are, just excuses – should be unacceptable.

The issue is complicated even further by the fact that many managers and employees really believe that their fire-fighting efforts are only being applied to new fires. But through interviews, it has become clear that many people are spending (or wasting) valuable time trying to sort out the same problems over and over again. This seems to stem from the multiple beliefs that: (a) if you haven't had a go at the problem in the past, it is a new problem; (b) if the problem hasn't been seen in a while, it counts as a new problem; and (c) if there is a slight variation in the way the problem manifests itself, it also counts as a new problem. And fighting new fires is deemed to be an acceptable behaviour.

I do want to make something extremely clear here: I completely agree that organizational fires need to be put out. However,

I struggle to understand how it can be rationalized for managers and/or employees to be putting effort on trying to solve the same problems over and over again.

The cost of fire-fighting the same fires over and over again can be tremendous, and some of this cost is directly monetary (lost time that could be spent improving performance, working to meet customer needs, or otherwise focused on satisfying a company mission). But the indirect cost to an organization can be even higher.

Organizations in which repetitive fire-fighting is condoned (and valued) tend to have lower morale, less commitment to the achievement of organizational goals, and a less-than-complimentary view of senior management. This is because the employees *know* that the problems have been there over time and would like to contribute to something more effective than having to fix someone else's reccurring problem.

Until management can come to the realization of the real cost of inappropriate fire-fighting efforts, this pattern of behaviour will remain a drag on business. Therefore, it is appropriate to help them understand what managers and employees are really doing with their time spent on problem solving. A simple 2×2 matrix can be used to do this.

The matrix is laid out with 'High value' written on the top, 'Low value' on the bottom, 'New issues, challenges and problems' on the right side, and 'Old issues, challenges and problems' on the left side. Participants in the process are then asked to place a symbol in the quadrant that most clearly approximates where they spend their problem-solving time.

The key to using this matrix is in the understanding of the titles. 'New issues, challenges and problems' means something that the organization has never seen before. Not just new to that person, not just sort of new, and not just new this month . . . new means it has never caused a problem in the past. 'Old' means that the organization has experienced this problem in the past at some point, and regardless if the problem has been tackled previously, if you have seen it before, it is an old problem. 'High value' and 'Low value' are relative terms. In some organizations, 'High value' may mean anything over £5,000, but in some others, it might mean anything over £5,000,000. Just pick some arbitrary amount and let everyone participating know what high and low mean for this exercise.

In the sample shown in Figure 32, the participants were asked to note where they were spending their time (the square shapes), as

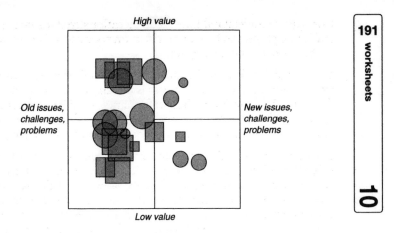

Figure 32

well as where they thought the balance of their organizations were spending their problem-solving time (the circular shapes). The fact that some of the various shapes are different sizes is simply a reflection of how big the participant actually drew his or her shapes.

The matrix shown is a composite of all the participants' matrices, and can be used to provide a good view of where the participants (in this example, a production team) and the organization had been spending their problem-solving time. And as can be seen in the sample, too many people are spending too much time duplicating efforts of previous problem-solving attempts.

A variation of using this worksheet would be to enquire as to what percentage of time is actually being spent on fire-fighting, and then multiply that percentage times the cost to keep the person employed by the company . . . but that number, whilst a clear reflection of how much time and money is being wasted, could be too depressing to think about.

The full size template of the matrix shown in Figure 33 can be found at www.rieley.com, Resources link.

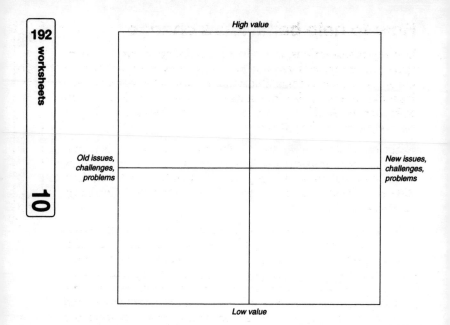

Figure 33

How to help behaviours change

In many organizations, it has become quite apparent that managers and employees are not even sure how their behaviours impact the organizational ability to deal with change and crises. It should be equally clear that if they are to be able to evolve them to become more effective (and less reactive), they need to have a structure that can help them.

Behaviours in organizations are largely a function of personal and collective competencies. And regardless of what competency metrics organizations use, there really are only four that make a difference. These four competencies are: Thinking, Influencing, Achieving and Leading.

- Thinking – how managers and employees formulate responses to various stimuli; how they identify opportunities and challenges; and how they see themselves in the organizational structure.
- Influencing – how managers and employees interact with others, both internally and externally; how they help to create and build alignment around mission, goals and targets; and how they create environments in which other managers and employees can be inspired to demonstrate high performance.
- Achieving – how managers and employees deliver performance; how they manage others; and how they achieve organizational goals and targets.
- Leading – how managers and employees demonstrate leadership in team and departmental environments; how they share organizational vision; and how they create environments in which other managers and employees can realize their individual and collective potential.

All four of these competencies are critical if an organization is to be able to be effective in an environment of change, and to survive through organizational crises.

Organizational behaviours, both personal and collective, cannot be changed. However, through the utilization of the Change Worksheet, managers and employees can have the opportunity to change them. This may seem like just playing games with words, but the reality is that behaviours do not change sustainably through mandate. But if managers and employees *choose* to change them, this can be accomplished. The Change Worksheet was developed to enable this to occur.

The worksheet looks like (another) matrix, with the four competencies listed across the top of the vertical rows (see the example in Figure 34). On the left, change or crisis behavioural issues are listed in rows. Users of the worksheet are asked to fill in the matrix cells with what they believe they can do in order to shift the way they think about these issues; what they can do to better influence others to accept the changes and avoid the problems associated with organizational crises; what they could do to shift the way in which they achieve organizational goals and targets when faced with ongoing change and potential crises; and how they can better demonstrate their ability to lead in these environments. The key is to have the users write in *what they believe they can do*, and inherent in having them describe what they *can do*, is that because they wrote the behavioural modifications themselves, they *will* do them.

In this process, it is important to ensure that the users know that what they write will become part of their performance review. The logic for this is clear – you said you would do this, but have you done it? In many cases where this Change Worksheet has been used, peers or direct reports are asked at a later date if they have actually seen these new behaviours being demonstrated. In some cases, the answers have been yes, but I have seen other cases where a manager will say that he has exhibited the new behaviours, but if no one has seen them, then the behaviours have not been demonstrated. And demonstrating behaviours is what behavioural change is all about. This process has been written about in depth in *Leadership* (Rieley, Hodder, 2006) under the title 'The Journey to Z'.

An option for the Change Worksheet is, after the users have filled out all the matrix cells (usually this can be accomplished in less than 30 minutes or can be done overnight and turned in the following day), he (or she) is given another copy of the worksheet, but this one has the addition of the following words in each matrix cell: 'what can I do more of' and 'what can I do less of'. The objective being that once the user has filled out each of the cells with what he *could do* differently, he is now given the opportunity to recognize what behaviours he currently demonstrates, in the context of what he says he can do, he can improve upon. If he thinks that he does some things well, he would probably say he would do more of them; but if, based on what he believes he could do, he thinks he is demonstrating some behaviours that are not helpful, he would probably say he would do less of them.

The full size template of the worksheet shown in Figure 35 can be found at www.rieley.com, Resources link.

	Behaviours			
	Thinking	Influencing	Achieving	Leading
Ongoing change initiatives	– I will try to understand better the need for the initiatives and how they may influence my team's performance.	– I will help my team deal with any added workload demands they may have due to the ongoing initiatives, and if their workloads are too high, I will lobby for additional support for the team.	– I will ensure that my and my team's goals are not neglected because of ongoing (and never-ending) change initiatives by helping them better prioritize their time.	– I will ensure that my team knows that we are all in this together and that I believe that the initiatives will add value to the organization and make their work lives easier . . . eventually.
Potential our competition will outrun us	– I will work with our sales team to understand better our customers' needs and help them plan ways to make our offering better for our customers.	– I will work with our production team to help them get their heads around the competitive threat, and with my team to develop improved processes that we can deploy throughout the organization.	– I will ensure that my team has the resources needed to be able to deliver on our responsibilities, on time and in full.	– I will re-institute a training programme for my team that will enable them to have the skills they need to hit our deadlines and assist in the presentation of our programmes to senior management.
Risk of crippling government regulations	– I will research existing and contemplated regulations that may negatively impact my team's efforts.	– I will hold a planning session to obtain team members' views on how we can avoid creating problems for the organization by overstepping regulations.	– I will ensure that my team follows all current and contemplated regulations.	– I will volunteer to participate in organization-wide regulation responses, and immediately update my team on all changes, as well as providing training to meet all new regulatory standards.

Figure 34

Figure 35

	Thinking	Influencing	Achieving	Leading
Ongoing change initiatives				
Potential our competition will outrun us				
Risk of crippling government regulations				

Behaviours

Managing through change and crisis can be brutal, but in most cases, this is not due to circumstances that are beyond our control. Quite the opposite is true: research on the subject has shown that the central reasons for problems dealing with change are due to internal resistance to change, the limitations of existing organizational systems, lack of senior management commitment, the lack of a senior management champion for change, unrealistic expectations about what will happen and how, lack of cross-functional teams to implement it, a sense that change can be rushed, or that change is only an organizational programme that has a start and stop, and inadequate skills on the part of those dealing with the change. And because of these gaps, less than 10 per cent of organizations that believe they have put forth serious efforts to manage change believe that they have been successful. In short, most change problems are due to our seeming inability to understand change and deal with it effectively.

If you are serious about managing through change and crisis (or even more importantly, avoiding many of the crises that organizations suffer through), there are some things you can do.

1 Put conversations about change in the context of improving business performance.
2 Ensure that you have a good idea how managers and employees view change, and their readiness to accept it.
3 Have a plan to deal with change *before* you need it, and a plan means as robust a plan as you would develop for your strategy, because at the end of the day, your strategy must work in an ever-changing environment.
4 Continually increase the number of managers and employees who will be responsible for surviving change.

5 Ensure that everyone has a clear understanding of how the change will impact them and the organization as a whole. Explain how shifting behaviours will impact suppliers and customers.

6 Test decisions before they are implemented. Don't fall into the trap that just because something makes sense to you, it will make sense to everyone. Anticipate what some of the unintended consequences will be of your efforts to deal with change and crises.

7 Use teams to drive change, whilst at the same time, ensure that the teams have high-level support for their work.

8 Continually reinforce communications about change from all managerial levels.

9 Always be conscious that there will be part of your organizational population who may not fully understand the what, why, and how you will deal with change. Be conscious that some of your people may not have the skills needed to effectively survive change and crises. And be conscious that a small minority of your people will do whatever they can to game the system and desperately try to keep the status quo.

10 Be conscious that performance behaviours will probably get worse before they improve and that part of dealing with change and crises is to survive this dip in performance.

11 Don't fall into the trap of believing that surviving one crisis or another means that you will not have another one. Learn how to put crises in context – they will always be there; your challenge is learning how to deal with them effectively.

12 If you are in management, get out of the office and go talk to your people. No, even better, go *listen* to your people. Ask them how you can help them survive change and make it through some of the crises the organization has been enduring easier. Listening doesn't mean just hearing the words; listen for what is behind those words.

13 Differentiate your organization from the competition. If your company can better differentiate itself, it will help you avoid some of the crises that arise from risking customer defection. Find out what your organization does best, and embed it as part of the organizational culture. Find out what it doesn't do well, and learn how to do it better. Yes, this may require more changing behaviours, but once you get it right, you will be in a better place and not subject to some of the crises of the past.

index

accountability, and addiction to
organizational change 31,
33, 35
Achieving, and the Change
worksheet 193, 195, 196
acquisitions and mergers 20, 22
and rationale for change 26
active participation in changing
96–8
addiction to organizational
change 28–35
Affinity Process 129
airline industry, and fast growth
45–6, 47
alignment
lack of in organizational goals
135
matrix 139–43, 181–3
and outsourcing 149
America On-Line (AOL) 98–9
American Revolution 11
AOL (America On-Line) 98–9
Arachnid Charts 129
Argyris, Chris 93, 153, 177
awareness, and evidence-based
coaching 81

BA (British Airways) 89–90, 99
bad news *see* good news/bad
news paradox
banks, lending money to
businesses 102–4
Bannister, Roger 31
behavioural gaps, and crises 9

belief-based coaching 80
beliefs
decision-making based on 51,
54–6
impact of change on 67–90
Boards and CEOs 85–7
change not taken seriously
74–7
deciding who you are 77–9
differing perspectives 72–4
and employee perceptions
68–70
the manager as coach
79–82
and panjandrums 82–5
planning for the future
88–90
and risk prevention 70–2
and the Ladder of inference
169, 187–8
binary thinking 11–12, 70
Board of Directors
and CEOs 85–7
and hiring decisions 61, 63–4
and orderly transitions of
leadership 118
box-ticking 74–7
BP 89, 103
brainstorming 127–30
British Airways (BA) 89–90, 99
budget constraints, and stress
in the workplace 144,
145, 147
bunker mentality 169–70

causal loop diagrams **xii**
CEOs
  changing **117–19**
  and decision-making **53–4,
    55, 57–8**
  identifying structural tension
    173–5
  as organizational saviours **40**
  problems with the Board **85–7**
  tenure of **89**
change **17–35**
  avoiding inappropriate
    addiction to **28–35**
  avoiding unintended
    consequences of **148–50**
  creating an environment for
    10–16
  enabling **22–8**
  fear of **96–8**
  how it occurs **7**
  impact of beliefs on **67–90**
  impact of decisions on **39–66**
  impact of **18–22, 198**
  inhibiting ability to deal with
    155–7
  internal resistance to **197**
  lack of commitment to **197**
  making change easier to
    accept **65–6**
  the power of changing
    behaviours **77–9**
  testing before implementing
    198
change not taken seriously **74–7**
Change worksheet **193–6**
choices
  and decision-making **47–9**
    hiring decisions **61–4**
  and evidence-based coaching
    81
  learning to do things
    differently **52, 53**
  and panjandrums **84**
  and performance
    improvement **132**
coaching
  changing organizational
    culture **169**

and effective change **79–82**
Collins, Jim, and the saviour as
    hero dynamic **40, 41**
commitment
  and compliance **65–6**
  from employees **5**
  and organizational
    climate/culture **44**
communications
  engaging the workforce in the
    communications process
    155–7
  helping people to understand
    change **28**
  impact on change efforts **92–6**
  see also Left-Hand Column
competence **138–57**
  ability to deal with change
    and avoid crises **155–7**
  dealing with stress in the
    workplace **143–8**
  the four competencies **193**
  heading off crises **150–2**
  and impending crisis **134, 136**
  and outsourcing **148–50**
  skilled incompetence **153–5**
  understanding alignment gaps
    139–43
competitors
  differing from **198**
  licensing to produce a
    product **134, 135**
  paying attention to **4**
contingency plans **5, 98–100,
    110–12, 152**
cost-reduction programmes,
    and impending crisis **134,
    135–6**
costs
  energy costs **18–19, 21–2**
  and outsourcing **148–9**
  procurement staff and
    incentive programmes
    123–7
creativity, and incentive
    programmes **123**
crises
  avoiding **61, 155–7**

avoiding setting yourself up
for 117–19
coming out of nowhere
109–12
early warning signals of 150–2
how they occur 7–10
impending 133–7
and loss of organizational
talent 42–4
and quick-fix solutions 40–2
reducing the potential for
crises occurring 139–43
and too much success too
quickly 44–7
understanding 6–7
and wicked problems 51–8
CSRP (customer service
process response) 53–4
customers
banks and customer services
103
expanding the customer pie
121–2
outsourcing and customer
satisfaction 149, 150
paying attention to 4

DeBeers 122
decentralization, and rationale
for change 26
deciding who you are 77–9
decision making 39–66
avoiding crises 61–4
and brainstorming 128
compliance and commitment
65–6
and fast growth 44–7
and impending crisis 133–7
and leading by example
59–61
and loss of organizational
talent 42–4
making decisions too quickly
49–51
making decisions too slowly
49–51
not understanding available
options 47–9

quick-fix solutions 40–2
rationality in 148
testing decisions 5
and wicked problems 51–8
delegation worksheets
184–6
Diageo 99
differing perspectives 72–4
Diffusion of Innovation (Rogers)
24–5
diffusion theory of change
24–5
disasters, early warning signals
of 150–1
Disney organization 59
dysfunctional behaviours, and
team working 61, 63–4

early warning signals 150–2
easyGroup 45
easyJet 45, 46
economic issue forces of
change 15
effective change, coaching
employees 79–82
effectiveness, and addiction to
organizational change 31,
34
Einstein, A. 47
Eisner, Michael 59
email 22
empirical data, and
brainstorming 130
employees
appreciating efforts of 5
bearing the brunt of change
initiatives 109
change initiative groups, and
alignment matrices 140,
141–2, 181–3
and choices in decision-
making 48
coaching 79–82
and corporate
communications 92–6
and cuts in training
programmes 100–2
discarding 20–1

employees (*cont.*)
  engaging in the
    communications process
    155-7
  and the four competences **193**
  gaining commitment from **5**
  incentive programmes **123-7**
  and initiative deployment
    162-3
  leading by example **59-61**
  learning for **5**
  and loss of organizational
    talent **42-4**
  and orderly transitions of
    leadership **117**
  and organizational culture of
    getting things done **111**
  outsourcing and employee
    morale **149**
  perceptions of, and the
    impact of change **68-70**
  problems of introducing
    organizational change
    96-8
  retention problems **165-7**
  seeing the same picture **4**
  skill set enhancement
    programmes **15-16**
  and skilled incompetence
    154-5
  stress in the workplace **143-8**
  training in life saving **71**
  understanding capabilities of
    58
enabling change **22-8**
energy dependency, impact of
  18-19, 21-2
energy prices **96-7, 99, 103, 152**
environmental forces of change
  15
events, organizations driven by
  98-100
evidence-based coaching **80-2**
expanding the customer pie
  121-2
experience, applying to the
  decision-making process
  49

external forces of change **14,
  15, 23-4**

fast growth **44-7**
fax machines, and technological
  change **19, 22**
fear of change **96-8**
feedback, and managers **85**
The Fifth Discipline (Senge) **23,
  55**
financial decision-making, and
  structural tension **173-5**
finding out what we don't know
  120-37
  brainstorming **127-30**
  impending crisis **133-7**
  implicit challenges **130-3**
  incentives **123-7**
  knowing what we don't know
    121-3
fire-fighting **88, 110, 153,
  189-90**
  and risk prevention **71, 72**
flexibility, and smaller
  companies **78**
Foreign Office (FO) **153**
Forester, Jay **23**
fork in the road scenario **72**
four competencies **193**
fractionalization in organizations
  12-14
future planning **88-90**

Gallwey, Tim, on
  evidence-based coaching
  80-2
gaming the system **9**
Gate Gourmet **99**
GEC-Marconi **89**
German elections (2005) **96**
getting the work done **107-19**
  crises coming out of nowhere
    109-12
  orderly transitions **117-19**
  and organizational structure
    114-17
  realizing the potential of
    teams **112-14**

senior managers and
      openness to change
      108–9
'good' decision-making 50
good news/bad news paradox
      19, 20, 55, 95
Good to Great (Collins) 40, 41
Google 77
Grant, Collinson 153

Hack, Kelvin 55
Haji-Ionnaou, Stelios 45, 47
head-hunters, and loss of
      organizational talent 43
health and safety 71
Hewlett-Packard 77
hiring employees
   employee retention problems
      165–7
   hiring decisions 61–4
Hirst, Damien 68
horsepower, and organizational
      structure 116

IBM 77
identifying structural tension
      173–5
IIP (Investing in People)
      programmes 74, 76
inappropriate addiction to
      change, avoiding 28–35
incentive programmes,
      unintended
      consequences of 123–7
Influencing, and the Change
      Worksheet 193, 195, 196
influencing factors 91–104
   communications 92–6
   money 102–4
   organizational change 96–8
   organizations driven by events
      98–100
   training 100–2
initiatives
   deploying process 162–3
   non-completion of, and stress
      in the workplace 144,
      145–6, 147–8

Institute of Directors 88
internal marketing, compliance
      and commitment 65–6
interpersonal skills, and
      managers 137
Interrelationship Diagraphs 129
interviewers, and hiring
      decisions 62–3, 64
interviews, hiring employees 167
investment decisions, prioritizing
      171–3

key influencers, and
      commitment 66
knowing what we don't know
      121–3
knowing what your options are
      72–4

Ladder of inference 169, 187–8
large companies, and SMEs
      77–9
leadership
   behaviours 83–4
   competence, and impending
      crisis 134, 136
   leading by example 59–61
   and management 84
   orderly transitions of 117–19
   saviour as hero dynamic 40–2
   and skilled incompetence
      155
   union leaders and alignment
      matrices 140, 142
Leading, and the Change
      worksheet 193, 195, 196
learning
   prioritizing 5
   and systems dynamics 23
   to do things differently 52, 53
Left-Hand Column 169
   and corporate
      communications 93–5
   worksheet 177–80
life saving, training employees in
      71
lifetime employment, ending of
      the concept of 20–1, 22

Macmillan, Harold **98**
management, and leadership **84**
managers
    and brainstorming **128–9**
    as coaches **79–82**
    and employee perceptions on
        the impact of change
        68–70
    engaging in the
        communications process
        155–7
    and feedback **85**
    and the four competences
        193
    and initiative deployment
        162–3
    and interpersonal skills **137**
    leading by example **59–61**
    and orderly transitions of
        leadership **117, 118**
    and organizational structure
        116
    and performance metrics
        111
    and skill set enhancement
        programmes **15–16**
    and skilled incompetence
        153–5
    and structural tension **175**
    surviving change **197**
    talking and listening to people
        198
    see also senior managers
market share, loss of **151**
matrices
    alignment **139–42**
    and brainstorming **129–30**
MDs (managing directors), and
    wicked problems **55–6**
meetings
    discussing desired behaviours
        in **169**
    and the Left-Hand Column
        93–5, 177
memory see organizational
    memory
mental models
    and addiction to

    organizational change
        30–2, 34–5
    and alignment building **141–2**
    and brainstorming **128**
    changing **167–9**
    and communications **95**
    decision-making based on
        52–3, 54–7
    senior managers and
        openness to change **108**
    shifting to accept change **97**
    and team work **113**
mergers and acquisitions see
    acquisitions and mergers
Microsoft **50, 77**
Minto, Barbara **86**
mission, and organizational
    structure **115**
money
    banks and businesses **102–4**
    financial decision-making
        173–5
more leads to more **8**
motivation, and non-completion
    of initiatives **147**

not knowing **44**

oil embargo (1974), impact of
    18–19
oil prices **96–7, 99, 103, 152**
orderly transitions **117–19**
organizational alignment see
    alignment
organizational climate/culture
    23, 198
    changing **167–9**
    and early warning signals
        152
    and employees' commitment
        43
    informal checks of **170**
    and new CEOs **117–18**
    and new employees **167**
    and performance
        improvement **132**
organizational goals
    lack of alignment in **135**

and skilled incompetence **154**
organizational memory, loss of
    21, 31–2
organizational structure **114–17**
    and company mission and
        vision **115**
    designing and testing
        115–16
    and horsepower **116**
    and the right people in the
        right jobs **116**
    and team work **113**
outcomes, of initiative
    deployment **162**
'outsiders', bringing in **40–2**
outsourcing, problems with
    148–50

panjandrums **82–5**
peer support, and new
    employees **167**
peer-to-peer learning **157**
people
    investing in **74–7**
    managers and people skills
        116
people in organizations,
    attitudes to change **27–8**
People's Express **45–6, 47**
performance
    and addiction to
        organizational change **32,
        33, 34, 35**
    element of sustainable
        performance
        improvement **132**
    improvement, and coaching
        79–82
    indicators of **151**
    management impatience with
        improvements in **54**
    metrics **111, 165**
    pressure to improve **169–71**
    priority hierarchy of **131–2**
    structures that impact **161–75**
Personnel Today **153**
planning for the future **88–90**
plans for change **5, 197**

contingency plans **5, 98–100,
    110–12, 152**
    see also strategic planning
politics, and addiction to
    organizational change **35**
power, of large companies over
    SMEs **77–9**
power structures, and addiction
    to organizational change
    35
pressure to improve
    performance **169–71**
prioritizing investment decisions
    171–3
priority decisions **88–9**
problem solving
    changing organizational
        cultures **168–9**
    deploying initiatives **162–3**
    employee retention **166–7**
    and fire-fighting **189–90**
    and impending crisis **133–7**
    sales performance **164–5**
problem-solving matrix **189–92**
procurement staff, and incentive
    programmes **123–7**

questioning change **35**
quick decision-making **49–51**
quick-fix solutions
    employee retention problems
        166
    lagging sales performance
        163–5
    and organizational crises **40–2**
    see also fire-fighting

rationale for change **25–7**
    impact of not making **26**
    making concrete and often
        25–6
rationality in business
    decision-making **148**
reactive thinking **88, 130–1, 153**
    and stress in the workplace
        144
regulations, paying attention to
    4

resistance to change, dealing with 28

reward policies, and stress in the workplace 145

risk prevention, avoiding risks of not changing 70–2

robbing Peter to pay Paul 130–3

Rogers, Everett, on the diffusion of change 24–5

Roosevelt, Franklin 97

Royal Dutch Shell 89

Royal Mail 150

Ryanair 89

sales, lagging sales and quick-fix solutions 163–5

saviour as hero dynamic 40–2

self-importance, falling victim to our own 82–5

Senge, Peter 23, 55

senior managers
addiction to organizational change 29–30, 32–5
and alignment matrixes 140, 141, 142, 181–3
and commitment 65, 66
and communications 92–6
and cuts in training programmes 100–2
differing perspectives 72–4
and feedback 85
lack of commitment to change 197
and openness to change 108–9
and organizational culture of getting things done 111
and risk prevention 70–2
and stress in the workplace 144, 147–8

shifting the burden 71–2

short-term thinking 130–1
and stress in the workplace 144

Shuler, Professor Heinz 127–8

skill set enhancement programmes 15–16

skilled incompetence 153–5

skills
and hiring decisions 62, 63
and new employees 166, 167
and stress in the workplace 143, 144, 146
for surviving change and crises 198

slow decision-making 49–51

SMEs (small and medium enterprises)
and bank loans 102–3
and large companies 77–9
lessons to learn about 4–5

SMEs (small and medium enterprises) xi–xii

social dynamic forces of change 15

stock prices, and crises 8, 9

strategic planning
and brainstorming 129
and crises coming out of nowhere 109–12

stress in the workplace 143–8
and budget constraints 144, 145, 147
and burnout 143
employee complaints 143–4
and employee skills 143, 144, 146
and non-completion of initiatives 144, 145–6, 147–8
and organizational change 29–30
reducing stress of employees 146–7
and reward policies 145
and senior managers 144
and team work 144, 145, 147
and training 144, 145, 146

structural tension, identifying 173–5

structured thinking, and CEO to Board updates 86–7

success
organizational not divisional 136–7

problems of too much too
quickly **44–7**
supplier relationships, and
SMEs **78–9**
sustainable organizations, and
crises **8**
systems dynamics/thinking **23,
70, 165**
simulation model **27**

A Tale of Two Cities (Dickens) **10**
talent, loss of organizational
42–4
team work
deploying initiatives **162–3**
and dysfunctional behaviours
61, 63–4
realizing the potential of
112–14
and stress in the workplace
144, 145, 147
'strong' and 'weak' participant
members **114**
and success in decision
making **46–7**
technological change
and diffusion **24**
impact of **20, 22**
technological issue forces of
change **15**
testing decisions **5**
Thinking, and the Change
worksheet **193, 195, 196**
Thompson, Hunter S. **102**
time, planning organizational
change **14–15**
Total Quality Management
(TQM) **54**
training
cancelling training
programmes **100–2**
and investment decisions
171–3
helping people with skills to
make changes **28**
and rationale for change
26–7
and risk prevention **71–2**

skill set enhancement
programmes **15–16**
and stress in the workplace
144, 145, 146
transitions, orderly **117–19**
trust
and corporate
communications **93–4**
and evidence-based coaching
81–2
and impending crisis **134,
135–6**
tsunami (Boxing Day 2004)
150–1
turbulence in organizations **59,
60**

union leadership, and alignment
matrices **140, 142, 183**
United States
creation of an environment for
change **10–11**
People's Express airline **45–6**

values
and choices in decision-
making **48**
and wicked problems **51**
vision
and decision-making **57**
and different perspectives **72,
74**
and leading by example
59–60
and organizational structure
115
and performance
improvement **132**
successful achievement of **84**
and team work **113**
Vodafone **77**
Volkswagen **77**

Walter, Norbert **96**
Weinstock, Lord **89**
whiplash-like change,
organizations numbed by
52, 54

wicked problems **51–8**
worksheets **176–96**
   alignment matrix **181–3**
   Change worksheet **193–6**
   delegation **184–6**

Ladder of inference **187–8**
Left-Hand Column **177–80**
problem-solving matrix
   189–92
templates **xii**

setting up a small business
vera hughes and david weller

- Are you setting up a small business?
- Do you need help to define what you have to offer?
- Are you looking for guidance in marketing and finance?

Setting up a Small Business, now in its fourth edition, gives you clear, concise information and guidance in all aspects of setting up a small business, including legal requirements, IT, finance and staffing issues.

Vera Hughes and **David Weller** started their own business in 1980 and have a wide experience of many areas of commerce. In addition to the phenomenally successful **Setting up a Small Business** they have written a number of books on retailing.

| teach yourself | **small business health check**
anna hipkiss |

- Are you running a small business?
- Do you need help to assess and improve your performance?
- Do you want to plan for a successful future?

Small Business Health Check is a complete guide to monitoring your performance so far and building on your own and others' successes and mistakes to ensure growth and success for your business. It will help you to diagnose and act upon your company's strengths and weaknesses, drawing on real examples of common pitfalls and success tactics, to help you make your business whatever you want it to be.

Anna Hipkiss is a business consultant and author, with experience in a wide variety of industries.